PRAISE FOR *POPE FRANCIS TO GO*

"The world is thirsting for the gospel. Unfortunately, in recent times, the mainstream media has been polluting the streams of water that have been flowing out of Rome. As a result, countless Catholics read the words of Pope Francis only after his message has been garbled and misinterpreted. Thanks to Christopher West's new book, *Pope Francis to Go*, we can draw deeply from the well of the great heart of Pope Francis. Christopher's prayerful and powerful commentary on *The Joy of the Gospel* offers practical insights on not only how to share the good news, but more importantly, how to live it."

–Jason Evert
Author, Speaker, Cofounder of The Chastity Project

"What does Pope Francis's *The Joy of the Gospel* have to do with the Theology of the Body for which Christopher West is known? Everything. As evangelizers, we can't be answering questions no one is asking. But everyone is asking how they can fulfill their desires, find love, be happy, be fulfilled. Pope Francis's teaching dovetails exactly with the Theology of the Body, as Christopher West masterfully demonstrates."

–Sister Helena Burns, FSP
Author, Filmmaker, Theology of the Body Presenter

"Christopher West shows how Pope Francis, with his own unique style, speaks in continuity with the great insights of St. John Paul II and Pope

Benedict XVI, shining new light on how to communicate hard Gospel truths in today's cultural climate. This is a must-read for anyone working in the New Evangelization!"

–Dr. Greg Popcak
Executive Director, Pastoral Solutions Institute, Author of Broken Gods: Hope, Healing, and the Seven Longings of the Human Heart

"Once again, Christopher West delivers a wonderful 'sampler' of papal thoughts for believers to easily access and chew over even in the midst of the busyness of daily life. Whoever takes pause and even for five minutes allows themselves time to daily ponder these gems of Pope Francis will be richly rewarded. The joy of the Gospel, concentrated so powerfully in this little book, will bring new strength and hope!"

–Bill Donaghy
Curriculum Specialist, Instructor, Speaker, Theology of the Body Institute

"In *Pope Francis to Go*, Christopher West packages Pope Francis's teaching into small grab bags that are perfect for our sound-bite culture. It provides essential quotes for teachers, Catholic journalists like myself, and all the faithful who want to spread Francis's message but don't have the time to take a highlighter through *The Joy of the Gospel*."

–Katie Breidenbach
Reporter, NET-TV (Brooklyn, NY)

"WOW! What a privilege to read *Pope Francis to Go*. I know I will treasure, pray with, and refer to it again and again for guidance and inspiration. It's a book I am excited to share with my friends—among whom are some tireless and dedicated evangelists and clergy—who love Pope Francis but who are unfamiliar with the Theology of the Body. This little book gives us marvelous common ground upon which to share."

–Mary Valla
Theology of the Body Student

"Christopher's reflections in *Pope Francis to Go* may contain some of the best clarity that he has ever written with. It truly speaks to the New Evangelization with a profound impact and with precise steps that are echoed in my own prayer life. Being affirmed here in the 'field hospital' at Marriage Missionaries doing triage, Christopher's understanding has reinvigorated our own calling. So grateful to God!"

–Matt Dalton
Cofounder of Marriage Missionaries (Colorado)

"*Pope Francis to Go* makes the purpose and way of evangelization so clear. As I read it I feel the joy of the Lord and I'm inspired to evangelize and share this book."

–Josephine Hamad
Theology of the Body Student

POPE FRANCIS TO GO

Bite-Sized Morsels from
The Joy of the Gospel

Arranged with Commentary by

Christopher West

Published in the United States by The Cor Project
corproject.com

ISBN: 978-0-9863543-0-4

Cover design and layout by Jay Ezell
studiojpxe.com

First edition

ABBREVIATIONS

AHG *At the Heart of the Gospel: Reclaiming the Body for the New Evangelization,* **Christopher West (Image, 2012)**

BNA *"Be Not Afraid,"* **André Frossard In Conversation with John Paul II (Image Books, 1985)**

BSCT *The Beatitudes: Soundings in Christian Tradition,* **Simon Tugwell O.P. (Templegate, 1980)**

CCC *Catechism of the Catholic Church* **(Libreria Editrice Vaticana, 1997)**

DC *Deus Caritas Est,* **Pope Benedict XVI's Encyclical Letter** *God Is Love* **(Pauline, 2006)**

EG *Evangelii Gaudium,* **Pope Francis's Apostolic Exhortation** *The Joy of the Gospel* **(Pauline, 2013)**

EV *Evangelium Vitae,* **John Paul II's Encyclical Letter** *The Gospel of Life* **(Pauline, 1995)**

FC *Familiaris Consortio,* **John Paul II's Apostolic Exhortation on the Role of the Christian Family in the Modern World (Pauline, 1981)**

FS *Through the Year with Bishop Fulton Sheen,* **Henry Dieterich (Ignatius Press, 2003)**

FTH *Fill These Hearts: God, Sex, and the Universal Longing,* **Christopher West (Image, 2013)**

GS *Gaudium et Spes,* **Vatican II's Pastoral Constitution on the Church in the Modern World (Pauline, 1965)**

LF *Letter to Families,* **John Paul II's Letter to Families in the Year of the Family (Pauline, 1994)**

LW   *Light of the World,* **Pope Benedict XVI (Ignatius Press, 2010)**

MCS   *Mary: The Church at the Source,* **Hans Urs von Balthasar and Joseph Cardinal Ratzinger (Ignatius Press, 2005)**

NE   *The New Evangelization,* **Joseph Cardinal Ratzinger's Address to Catechists, Dec. 12, 2000**

NMI   *Novo Millennio Ineunte,* **John Paul II's Apostolic Letter at the Close of the Great Jubilee (Pauline, 2001)**

RG   *The Reed of God,* **Caryll Houselander (Ave Maria Press, 2006)**

RH   *Redemptor Hominis,* **John Paul II's Encyclical Letter** *The Redeemer of Man* **(Pauline, 1979)**

SM   *The Secret of Mary,* **St. Louis de Montfort, adapted by Eddie Doherty (Montfort Publications, 1998)**

SP   *The Spirit,* **Volume III of John Paul II's Catechesis on the Creed (Pauline, 1996)**

SS   *Spe Salvi,* **Pope Benedict XVI's Encyclical Letter** *Saved in Hope* **(Pauline, 2007)**

TD   *True Devotion to the Blessed Virgin,* **St. Louis de Montfort (Montfort Publications, 1993)**

TOB   *Man and Woman He Created Them: A Theology of the Body,* **John Paul II's general audience addresses on Human Love in the Divine Plan (Pauline, 2006)**

VP   *Via Pulchritudinis (The Way of Beauty): Privileged Pathway for Evangelization and Dialogue,* **Pontifical Council for Culture (2006)**

CONTENTS

INTRODUCTION:
PURPOSE OF THIS BOOK

Since the moment the new pope took the name Francis and stepped out on the loggia (the central balcony) at St. Peter's Basilica, something new, something fresh seemed to be unfolding. That original intuition has only been confirmed since. The pope—who wears old brown shoes, forfeited the papal apartment, prefers to be driven in an economy car, gives off-the-cuff interviews, makes random personal phone calls to unsuspecting "commoners," and emphasizes incessantly his desire for a Church that is "poor" and "for the poor"—has certainly made an impression on the world stage.

But has the world, or the Church for that matter, taken the time to "ponder in its heart" what Francis actually has to say? We've heard the sound bites in the headlines and on the evening news, but have we gotten beyond the "spin" and gone to the source? This little "reflection book" is intended to help you do just that.

His marvelous document *The Joy of the Gospel*—an Apostolic Exhortation on the proclamation of the Gospel in today's world—represents his most extensive papal teaching to date. Unlike his encyclical letter *The Light of Faith,* which was primarily the voice of his predecessor, *The Joy of the Gospel* is pure Francis and offers the first extended, well-thought-out look into the heart and "style" of the first pope from the New World.

I knew this extensive papal reflection on the new evangelization would prove helpful for a class I teach on that subject. As I read through the document, I started pulling key quotes and organizing them topically as a supplement to the course materials I provide my students. I soon realized it was amounting to more than a "supplement" to my course: this was a resource that, with a little commentary to set the stage of each topic, could and should stand on its own.

That's what you now hold in your hands: 150 bite-sized morsels from Pope Francis's *The Joy of the Gospel* (a few are repeated because they pertain to more than one chapter heading). The two-part structure and the topical chapter headings are mine—the result of sorting all of the wisdom I pulled from Francis's document. Francis's quotes are referenced by paragraph number and are clearly set aside from the introductory comments in each chapter so that they can stand alone and speak for themselves.

Don't be fooled by the "to go" title, as if the point were to rush through the contents of this book. Rather, I wanted to make Pope Francis's wisdom accessible to those who might not have the time to sift through this document in its entirety. The morsels I've chosen are rich. Like cheesecake, you don't want to eat too much in one sitting. I'd suggest reading no more than one chapter at a time or, if you really want to "savor" the Holy Father's wisdom, perhaps just meditate on one or two quotes per day. You'll notice that some chapters are significantly shorter than others. Length should not be considered a measure of importance, however. None of these papal gems should be glossed over. Each repays careful attention.

Francis observes that ministers of the new evangelization "should appear as people who wish to share their joy, who point to a horizon of beauty, and who invite others to a delicious banquet" (EG 15). That's my intention of putting this little book together: to share the joy, point to the beauty, and invite you to the delicious banquet I've discovered in Pope Francis's teaching. *Bon appetit!*

PART I:
THE NEW EVANGELIZATION

CHAPTER 1:
DESIRE FOR GOD

The *Catechism of the Catholic Church* not only provides a comprehensive summation of the Catholic Faith. In its very structure, it also provides a methodology for sharing that faith with others. Where does the *Catechism* begin? *Desire.*

The first paragraph of Chapter One of Part One of the *Catechism* states: "The desire for God is written in the human heart, because man is created by God and for God; and God never ceases to draw man to Himself. Only in God will he find the truth and happiness he never stops searching for" (CCC 27). Left to himself, all man has in his heart is an abyss of sadness, and "infinite sadness can only be cured by an infinite love," says Pope Francis (EG 265). That infinite love is the ultimate object of human *desire.*

If the new evangelization is to succeed, we need what Pope Benedict described as a "pedagogy of desire"—a new education in the nature, meaning, and purpose of human *longing*. The secular world continually encourages us to take our desires to "false paradises," as Pope Benedict puts it. Within the Church, however, we often have the impression that following Christ means repressing, ignoring, or otherwise annihilating our desires. Quite the contrary! As Pope Benedict insists, Christianity is not "about suffocating the longing that dwells in the heart of man, but about freeing it, so that it can reach its true height" (November 7, 2012). And that "true height" is nothing short of infinite bliss, infinite joy, infinite ecstasy in union with God *forever.*

The Greeks had a word for this restless longing we all feel for infinite happiness and satisfaction: *eros.* Unfortunately, our English derivitave—*"erotic"*—often connotes a lustful desire for base pleasure. Our fallen humanity, indeed, tends to pull eros in that direction. Thanks be to God that Christ, as St. John Paul II wrote, enables us to reclaim "that fullness of 'eros,' which implies the upward impulse of the human spirit toward what is true, good, and beautiful, so that what is 'erotic' also becomes true, good, and beautiful" (TOB 48:1).

As the distortions of eros are untwisted, we discover once again that erotic longing is the desire in us that seeks something "more" than this world has to offer; it seeks a transcendent, infinite love; it seeks an eternal paradise. As Pope Benedict puts it, eros is the desire in us that "seeks God" (see DC 7).

Despite all the widespread impressions to the contrary, we must impress this truth upon our souls and let it settle in our bones: Christianity is the religion of desire—the religion that *redeems eros*—and its saints are the ones who have had the courage to *feel* that abyss of longing within them, and more importantly, learned how to direct that longing toward the One who alone can fulfill it.

And this means all true evangelization must appeal to eros—that "ache," that "cry," that "hunger" of the human heart for the infinite. As I once heard it said, evangelization is simply one hungry person showing another hungry person where to find bread.

FROM *THE JOY OF THE GOSPEL*

1 "Instead of seeming to impose new obligations, [ministers of the new evangelization] should appear as people who wish to share their joy, who point to the horizon of beauty, and who invite others to a delicious banquet" (15).

2 Humanity has a "deep, religious sense. We must examine this more closely in order to enter into a dialogue like that of our Lord and the Samaritan woman at the well where she sought to quench her thirst (see Jn 4:1–15)" (72).

3 (Quoting Pope Benedict XVI) In "'today's world there are innumerable signs, often expressed implicitly or negatively, of the thirst for God, for the ultimate meaning of life. And in the desert people of faith are needed who, by the example of their own lives, point out the way to the Promised Land and keep hope alive.' In these situations we are called to be living sources of water from which others can drink. At times, this becomes a heavy cross, but it was from the cross, from his pierced side, that our Lord gave himelf to us as a source of living water" (87).

4 "Today, our challenge is not so much atheism as the need to respond adequately to many people's thirst for God, lest they try to satisfy it with alienating solutions or with a disembodied Jesus who demands nothing of us with regard to others. Unless these people find in the Church a spirituality which can offer healing and liberation, and fill them with life and peace, while at the same time summoning them to fraternal communion and missionary fruitfulness, they will end up being taken in by solutions which neither make life truly human nor give glory to God" (89).

5 "All Christian formation consists of entering more deeply into . . . the message capable of responding to the desire for the infinite which abides in every human heart" (165).

6 The Gospel "responds to our deepest needs, since we were created for what the Gospel offers us: friendship with Jesus and love for our brothers and sisters. If we succeed in expressing adequately and with beauty the essential content of the Gospel, surely this message will speak to the deepest yearnings of people's hearts" (265).

7 (Quoting St. John Paul II) "'The missionary is convinced that, through the working of the spirit, there already exists in individuals and peoples an expectation, even if an unconscious one, of knowing the truth about God, about man, and about how we are to be set free from sin and death. The missionary's enthusiasm in proclaiming Christ comes from the conviction that he is responding to that expectation'" (265).

8 "Jesus' whole life, his way of dealing with the poor, his actions, his integrity, his simple daily acts of generosity, and finally his complete self-giving, is precious and reveals the mystery of his divine life. Whenever we encounter this anew, we become convinced that it is what

POPE FRANCIS TO GO

others need, even though they may not recognize it: 'What therefore you worship is unknown, this I proclaim to you' (Acts 17:23)" (265).

9 "Enthusiasm for evangelization is based on [the conviction that we] have a treasure of life and love which cannot deceive, and a message which cannot mislead or disappoint. It penetrates to the depths of our hearts, sustaining and ennobling us. It is a truth which is never out of date because it reaches that part of us which nothing else can reach. Our infinite sadness can only be cured by infinite love" (265).

CHAPTER 2:
THE FUNDAMENTAL MESSAGE

The Bible is a love story. As Pope Francis declares: "We, the women and men of the Church, we are in the middle of a love story; each of us is a link in the chain of love. And if we do not understand this, we have understood nothing of what the Church is" (April 24, 2013).

But what kind of love story is it? God loves us as a father, as a brother, and as a friend to be sure. However, the interpretive key that really unlocks the mystery of divine love is *marriage.* Indeed, from beginning to end, the Bible tells the story of the Bridegroom and of the Bride and of their longing to become "one."

The Bible begins with the marriage of man and woman, it ends with the marriage of Christ and the Church, and right in the middle of the biblical story we have the unabashed celebration of spousal union in the *Song of Songs.* The erotic poetry of the Song points ultimately to divine love and demonstrates that Christ loves his Church as "a lover with all the passion of true love," wrote Pope Benedict. Indeed, throughout the Old Testament, the prophets "described God's passion for His people using boldly erotic images" (DC 9, 10).

In the New Testament, the marriage of God and humanity is consummated in the "bridal chamber" of Mary's womb. Christ's first miracle is at a wedding. He calls himself the "Bridegroom." And at the high point of the entire biblical analogy of spousal love, St. Paul describes the "one flesh" union of spouses as a "great mystery" that refers to Christ and the Church (see Eph 5:31–32). This "great mystery," St. John Paul II tells us, is "the central theme of the whole of revelation, its central reality. It is what God . . . wishes above all to transmit to mankind in his Word" (TOB 93:2).

What does God wish "above all" to transmit in his Word? He loves us. He loves us as a father, and brother, and friend, to be sure. But he loves us in a particular way as a Spouse. In fact, we could summarize the entire Bible with these five words: "God wants to marry us." When we proclaim Christ's saving love to others, we are proclaiming the love of the eternal Bridegroom for his Bride and we are inviting them into this eternal communion with the divine.

"It is emblamatic," says Pope Francis, "how in the *Book of Revelation,* John, taking up the intuition of the Prophets, describes the final, definitive dimension [of our existence] in terms of 'the new Jerusalem, coming down out of heaven from God, prepared as a bride adorned for her husband' (Rev 21:2). Here is what awaits us!" exclaims Francis. "And here, then, is who the Church is . . . a bride with her bridegroom. And it is not just a matter of speaking: they will be real and true nuptials! Yes, because Christ . . . has truly wed us and has made us, as a people, his bride. This is nothing more than the fulfillment of the plan of communion and love woven by God throughout history . . . " (October 15, 2014).

Being a Christian, then, does not mean learning how to abide by a set of dry doctrines and repressive rules. It means learning how to direct the deepest longing of our hearts (eros) toward that which truly satisfies: the eternal marriage of Christ and the Church. These "heavenly nuptials" are what we yearn for, what we're created for, and what we're destined for. This is "the message capable of responding to the desire for the infinite which abides in every heart," to use Pope Francis's expression (EG 265). If Christianity is not framed as such—as God's passionate desire for union with us and our quest for the true satisfaction of eros in union with him—it eventually becomes incomprehensible and even meaningless. More than that, it can even morph into something destructive to our true humanity (see FTH, p. 102).

What is the task, then, of the new evangelization? It's nothing other than heeding Christ's call to "go into the main streets and invite everyone to the wedding feast" (Mt 22:9).

FROM *THE JOY OF THE GOSPEL*

10 "When we adopt a pastoral goal and a missionary style which would actually reach everyone without exception or exclusion, the message has to concentrate on the essentials, on what is most beautiful, most grand, most appealing and at the same time most necessary. The message is simplified, while losing none of its depth and truth, and thus becomes all the more forceful and convincing" (35).

11 "All revealed truths derive from the same divine source, and are to be believed with the same faith, yet some of them are more import-ant for giving direct expression to the heart of the Gospel. In this basic core, what shines forth is the beauty of the saving love of God made manifest in Jesus Christ who died and rose from the dead" (36).

12 (Quoting St. John Paul II) There "'can be no true evangeliza-tion without the explicit proclamation of Jesus as Lord,' and without the primacy of the proclamation of Jesus Christ in all evangelization work" (110).

13 Evangelizers must always keep "in mind the fundamental message: the personal love of God who became man, who gave himself up for us, who is living and who offers his salvation and his friendship. This message has to be shared humbly as a testimony on the part of one who is always willing to learn, in the awareness that the message is so rich and so deep that it always exceeds our grasp. At times the message can be presented directly, at times by way of a personal witness or gesture, or in a way which the Holy Spirit may suggest in that particular situation" (128).

14 The "first proclamation must ring out over and over: 'Jesus Christ loves you; he gave his life to save you; and now he is living at your side every day to enlighten, stengthen and free you.' This first proclamation is . . . the one which we must hear again and again in different ways, the one which we must announce one way or another throughout the process of catechesis, at every level and moment" (164).

15 "All Christian formation consists of entering more deeply into the kerygma [the first and fundamental proclamation of God's infinite love] which is reflected in and constantly illumines the work of catechesis [ongoing Christian education] . . . . It is the message capable of responding to the desire for the infinite which abides in every human heart" (165).

16 The first proclamation "has to express God's saving love which precedes any moral and religious obligation on our part; it should not impose the truth but appeal to freedom; it should be marked by joy, encouragement, liveliness and a harmonious balance which will not reduce preaching to a few doctrines which are at times more philosophical than evangelical. All this demands on the part of the evangelizer certain attitudes which foster openness to the message: approachability, readiness for dialogue, patience, a warmth and welcome which is non-judgmental" (165).

17 "Helping our people to feel that they live in the midst of [the embrace of the Father that he gave us in baptism and the embrace of the Father that awaits us in glory] is the difficult but beautiful task of one who preaches the Gospel" (144).

CHAPTER 3:
EVANGELISTS

In order to understand the disposition of a true evangelist, we must understand what the *Catechism* means when it maintains that "the 'Marian' dimension of the Church precedes the 'Petrine'" (773).

The Petrine dimension refers to the Church's teaching office founded on Peter, the first pope. The Marian dimension refers to the Church's contemplative posture before the Lord founded on Mary, the Mother of God. The Petrine dimension emphasizes the "masculine" mode of *doing* while the Marian dimension emphasies the "feminine" mode of *letting* it be done.

Evangelists are called to share Christ with others. However, *we cannot give what we do not have.* And this means that evangelization is not first a matter of "doing" something, but, rather, of "letting it be done" unto us. In other words, if we are to teach others about Christ in union with Peter, we must first *receive* Christ in union with Mary. This

19

is why it is so critical that the Marian dimension precede the Petrine. If it doesn't, the message we share as evangelists will be "our own" rather than "the Father's" (see Jn 7:16). In turn, we will "labor all night and catch nothing" (see Lk 5:5).

To summarize this principle, St. John Paul II appealed to a traditional Latin expression: *Contemplata aliis tradere,* which means, "hand on to others the fruits of prayer." This ancient principle, he said, "concerns in the first place the one who 'hands on,' the preacher or servant of the word: he is entitled to communicate . . . only *contemplata,* thoughts passed through prayer" (BNA, p. 33). Pope Francis puts it this way: evangelists must allow God's word to "enter their own hearts before then passing it on to others. Christ's message must truly penetrate and possess the preacher, not just intellectually but in his entire being" (EG 151).

Once again, Mary is our model here. She is the first to let Christ "possess her entire being." In a pre-papal essay, Pope Benedict XVI underscored the critical importance of this "Marian dimension" for the whole Church when he wrote that the:

> . . . connection between the mystery of Christ and the mystery of Mary . . . is very important in our age of activism, in which the Western mentality has evolved to the extreme. For in today's intellectual climate, only the masculine principle counts . . . . This attitude

characterizes our whole approach to the Church. We treat the Church almost like some technological device that we plan and make with enormous cleverness and expenditure of energy. Then we are surprised when we . . . "do much but nothing comes of it" (Hag 1:6)! . . . . The Church is not a manufactured item; she is, rather, the living seed of God that must be allowed to grow and ripen. This is why the Church needs the Marian mystery; this is why the Church herself is a Marian mystery. There can be fruitfulness in the Church only when she has this character, when she becomes holy soil for the Word. We must retrieve the symbol of the fruitful soil; we must once more become waiting, inwardly recollected people who in the depth of prayer, longing, and faith give the Word room to grow (MCS, pp. 15–17).

FROM *THE JOY OF THE GOSPEL*

18 An "evangelizer must never look like someone who has just come back from a funeral" (10)!

19 "Instead of seeming to impose new obligations, [ministers of the new evangelization] should appear as people who wish to share their joy, who point to a horizon of beauty, and who invite others to a delicious banquet" (15).

20 An evangelizing community (see 24):

- knows the Lord has taken the initiative by loving us first;
- has an endless desire to show mercy, the fruit of its own experience of God's mercy;
- gets involved in people's daily lives;
- embraces human life, touching the suffering flesh of Christ in others;
- takes on the "smell of the sheep";
- stands by people every step of the way, no matter how difficult or lengthy the journey;
- is familiar with patient expectation and apostolic endurance;
- disregards contraints of time;
- cares for the grain in its desire to bear fruit but does not grow impatient with weeds;
- does not grumble or overreact when weeds sprout among the grain;
- is ready to put its own life on the line, even to the point of martyrdom;
- is filled with joy and knows how to rejoice always;
- celebrates every victory, every step forward in the work of evangelization;
- has a daily concern to spread goodness, and;
- draws the source of its renewed self-giving from the beauty of the liturgy.

21 (Quoting Pope Benedict XVI) "'It is important always to know that the first word, the true initiative, the true activity comes from God, and only inserting ourselves into the divine initiative, only begging for this divine initiative, shall we too be able to become—with him and in him—evangelizers'" (112).

22 "The new evangelization calls for personal involvement on the part of each of the baptized. Every Christian is challenged, here and now, to be actively engaged in evangelization; indeed, anyone who has experienced God's saving love does not need much time or lengthy training to go out and proclaim that love . . . . Of course, all of us are called to mature in our work as evangelizers. We want to have a better training, a deepening love and a clearer witness to the Gospel. In this sense, we ought to let others be constantly evangelizing us. But this does not mean that we should postpone the evangelizing mission . . . . In your heart you know that it is not the same to live without him; what you have come to realize, what has helped you to live and given you hope, is what you also need to communicate to others. Our falling short of perfection should be no excuse" (120-121).

23 "The Church, in her commitment to evangelization, appreciates and encourages the charism of theologians and their scholarly efforts to advance dialogue with the world of cultures and sciences. I call on theologians to carry out this service as part of the Church's saving mission. In doing so, however, they must always remember that the Church and theology exist to evangelize, and not be content with a desk-bound theology" (133).

24 "We are not asked to be flawless, but to keep growing and wanting to grow as we advance along the path of the Gospel . . . . What is essential is that the preacher be certain that God loves him, that Jesus Christ has saved him and that his love always has the last word" (151).

25 If a preacher of the Gospel "does not take time to hear God's word with an open heart, if he does not allow it to touch his life, to challenge him, to impel him, and if he does not devote time to pray with that word, then he will indeed be a false prophet, a fraud, a shallow imposter" (151).

26 "The Lord wants to make use of us as living, free and creative beings who let his word enter their own hearts before then passing it on to others. Christ's message must truly penetrate and possess the preacher, not just intellectually but in his entire being" (151).

27 Authentic evangelization "demands on the part of the evangelizer certain attitudes which foster openness to the message: approachability, readiness for dialogue, patience, a warmth and welcome which is non-judgmental" (165).

28 The sacred Scriptures are the very source of evangelization. Consequently we need to be constantly trained in hearing the word. The Church does not evangelize unless she constantly lets herself be evangelized" (174).

29 Evangelizers must be "firmly rooted in prayer, for without prayer all our activity risks being fruitless and our message empty. Jesus wants evangelizers who proclaim the good news not only with words, but above all by a life transfigured by God's presence" (259).

30 Intercessory prayer is "a prayer of gratitude to God for others . . . . Far from being suspicious, negative and despairing, it is a spiritual gaze born of deep faith which acknowledges what God is doing in the lives of others" (282).

CHAPTER 4:
WHY WE EVANGELIZE

True evangelists share the Gospel with others not out of a sense of cold duty, but for one reason: "love is diffusive of itself," as the ancients put it. In other words, love wants to share itself, expand its own communion. That's why the God who "is love" created us in the first place: to expand his own communion beyond the exchange of Father, Son, and Holy Spirit to an expansive communion of saints, all sharing in the bliss the Persons of the Trinity have known eternally.

We evangelize because we have caught fire and we want the whole world to know the sweet burning of divine love.

We evangelize because we have woken up from our amnesia, we've discovered who we *really* are as human beings, and we long to share the true story of what it means to be human with others.

We evangelize because we've discovered the innermost secret of God—"God himself is an eternal exchange of love . . . and he has destined us to share in that exchange" (CCC 221)—and we long to let the whole world in on this secret.

We proclaim to others what we "have seen and heard" so that they also "may have fellowship with us. And our fellowship is with the Father and with his Son, Jesus Christ." We evangelize "to make our joy complete"—the joy of living for the love for which we are created (see 1 Jn 1:3–4).

We evangelize because we have found a living hope of the satisfaction of our deepest desires, and we long to invite everyone to the wedding feast!

Those who have tasted the living hope of this wedding feast feel compelled to invite others, like St. Paul: "woe to me if I do not preach the gospel" (1 Cor 9:16). If we do not feel compelled in this way, perhaps we are in need of being more deeply evangelized ourselves. That's okay, for at every stage of our journey we're in need of deeper conversion. If we continue to open our hearts ever more deeply to God's love, it will flow out of us with ever greater ease and naturalness.

But if this is to happen, as Pope Francis says below, we must have a contemplative spirit—a heart thirsting for divine love and eager to drink at its fountain, the open heart of Christ. In other words, we must learn how to *pray*. True evangelization is always and only the fruit of a deep life of prayer. For the "authenticity of the Christian life is measured by the depth of one's prayer," wrote St. John Paul II. Prayer is "an art that must be humbly learnt 'from the lips of the Divine Master,' almost imploring like the first disciples: 'Lord, teach us to pray' (Lk 11:1)" (April 17, 2005)!

This "wanting to learn how to pray" is especially important for the evangelist. As St. John of the Cross wrote:

> Let those, then, who are singularly active, who think they can win the world with their preaching and exterior works, observe here that they would profit the Church and please God much more . . . were they to spend at least half of this time with God in prayer . . . . They would then certainly accomplish more, and with less labor by one work than they otherwise would by a thousand . . . . Without prayer they would do a great deal of hammering but accomplish little, and sometimes nothing, and even at times cause harm . . . . However much they may appear to achieve externally, they will in substance be accomplishing nothing [without a life of deep prayer] (*Spiritual Canticle*, 29:3).

FROM *THE JOY OF THE GOSPEL*

31 "The unified and complete sense of human life that the Gospel proposes is the best remedy for the ills of our cities, even though we have to realize that a uniform and rigid program of evangelization is not suited to this complex reality" (75).

32 The "principle of universality [is] intrinsic to the Gospel, for the Father desires the salvation of every man and woman, and his saving plan consists in 'gathering up all things in Christ, things in heaven and things on earth' (Eph 1:10). Our mandate is to 'go into all the world and proclaim the good news to the whole creation' (Mk 16:15)" (181).

33 "The primary reason for evangelizing is the love of Jesus which we have received, the experience of salvation which urges us to ever greater love of him . . . . If we do not feel an intense desire to share this love, we need to pray insistently that he will once more touch our hearts. We need to implore his grace daily, asking him to open our cold hearts and shake up our lukewarm and superficial existence" (264).

34 "The best incentive for sharing the Gospel comes from contemplating it with love, lingering over its pages and reading it with the heart. If we approach it in this way, its beauty will amaze and constantly excite us. But if this is to come about, we need to recover a contemplative spirit" (264).

35 "It is not the same thing to try to build the world with his Gospel as to try to do so by our own lights. We know well that with Jesus life becomes richer and that with him it is easier to find meaning in everything. This is why we evangelize" (266).

36 The conviction that we have a treasure to share with others "has to be sustained by our own constantly renewed experience of savoring Christ's friendship and his message. It is impossible to persevere in a fervent evangelization unless we are convinced from personal experience that it is . . . not the same thing to contemplate him, to worship him, to find our peace in him, as not to" (266).

37 "In union with Jesus, we seek what he seeks and we love what he loves. In the end, what we are seeking is the glory of the Father . . . . Beyond all our own preferences and interests, our knowledge and motivations, we evangelize for the greater glory of the Father who loves us" (267).

CHAPTER 5:
A MISSIONARY HEART

"As the Father has sent me, so I send you" (Jn 20:21). The Father "sent" (*missio*) Jesus to reveal to the world his eternal love. Jesus "sends" us in the same capacity. This is our *mission* as evangelists: "to bring to light what is the plan of the mystery hidden from ages past in God who created all things" (Eph 3:9).

What is that mystery we are to make known? Recall our summary of the whole Bible from Chapter 2: *God wants to marry us* . . . and, whether we realize it or not, *we want to marry him!* This is why we have all those *desires* in us (Chapter 1): we're created for an eternal marriage, for what the saints call "nuptial union"—*with God!* This eternal union is the North Pole to which our innermost compass is oriented. And that's why St. John Paul II tells us that inviting people to this eternal union is "the final and grandiose goal of all evangelization" (March 10, 1987).

To have a "missionary heart" is to have a heart filled with hope in the everlasting satisfaction of this union offered us in Christ and to want to venture beyond our self-enclosed and self-absorbed worlds to share this hope with others. As Pope Francis illuminates in the selection of quotes for this chapter, this takes courage, boldness, creativity, generosity, and a willingness to have our shoes get "soiled with the mud on the street" (EG 45).

A person with a missionary heart does not look at the world through binoculars. He doesn't stand at a distance from the sheep, but gets up close and "takes on their smell" (see EG 24). And when he finds one injured or one that has lost its way, he cares for it tenderly and with compassion. For he knows that he, too, is a wounded sheep in need of the tender care of others.

A person with a missionary heart knows well the difference between the sin and the sinner. He speaks always with clarity and charity. He knows that sin is a disordered attachment to something good (see CCC 1849), is able to affirm that good, and patiently helps a person redirect his desires (eros) toward the ultimate good (God) that alone can satisfy. And he does so without any hint of self-righteousness, superiority, or condemnation of others.

In short, a person with a missionary heart is a witness to hope. For hope is the virtue that orients our desire for happiness to that which alone can satisfy it (see CCC 1817–18).

FROM *THE JOY OF THE GOSPEL*

38 "I dream of a 'missionary option', that is, a missionary impulse capable of transforming everything, so that the Church's customs, ways of doing things, times and schedules, language and structures can be suitably channeled for the evangelization of today's world rather than for her self-preservation" (27).

39 "Pastoral ministry in a missionary key seeks to abandon the complacent attitude that says: 'We have always done it this way.' I invite everyone to be bold and creative in the task of rethinking the goals, structure, style, and methods of evangelization in their respective communities . . . . I encourage everyone to apply the guidelines found in this document generously and courageously, without inhibitions or fear" (33).

40 "The task of evangelization operates within the limits of language and circumstances. It constantly seeks to communicate more effectively the truth of the Gospel in a specific context . . . . A missionary heart is aware of these limits and makes itself 'weak with the weak . . . everything for everyone' (1 Cor 9:12)" (45).

41 "A missionary heart . . . never closes itself off, never retreats into its own security, never opts for rigidity and defensiveness. It realizes that it has to grow in its own understanding of the Gospel and in discerning the paths of the Spirit, and so it always does what good it can, even if in the process its shoes get soiled by the mud of the street" (45).

42 "Pastoral ministry in a missionary style is not obsessed with the disjointed transmission of a multitude of doctrines to be insistently imposed. When we adopt a pastoral goal and a missionary style which would actually reach everyone without exception or exclusion, the message has to concentrate on the essentials, on what is most beautiful, most grand, most appealing and at the same time most necessary. The message is simplified, while losing none of its depth and truth, and thus becomes all the more forceful and convincing" (35).

43 "Interreligious dialogue is in first place a conversation about human existence or simply . . . a matter of 'being open to [others], sharing their joys and sorrows.' In this way we learn to accept others and their different ways of living, thinking, and speaking" (250). "True openness involves remaining steadfast in one's deepest convictions, clear and joyful in one's own identity, while at the same time being 'open to understanding those of the other party' and 'knowing that dialogue can enrich each side'" (251).

44 "A true missionary . . . never ceases to be a disciple, knows that Jesus walks with him, speaks to him, breathes with him, works with him. He senses Jesus alive with him in the midst of the missionary enterprise. Unless we see him present at the heart of our missionary commitment, our enthusiasm soon wanes and we are no longer sure of what it is that we are handing on; we lack vigor and passion. A person who is not convinced, enthusiastic, certain and in love, will convince nobody" (266).

45 "If we want to advance in the spiritual life, then, we must constantly be missionaries . . . . A committed missionary knows the joy of being a spring which spills over and refreshes others. Only the person who feels happiness in seeking the good of others, in desiring their happiness, can be a missionary" (272).

CHAPTER 6:
MISSIONARY FRUITFULNESS

As we've been saying repeatedly already, the primary biblical image for comprehending the divine mystery is marriage—the lifelong union of one man and one woman in "one flesh." Marriage also provides, therefore, the primary image of missionary fruitfulness.

Whenever God establishes a covenant with his people, whether it is with Adam (Gen 1:28), Noah (Gen 9:1), Abraham (Gen 17:5–6), Jacob (Gen 35:10–12), or Moses (Lev 26:9), we see the call to be "fruitful and multiply." Indeed the very promise of the Old Covenant was marital fruitfulness: "Behold my covenant is with you, and you shall be the father of a multitude of nations . . . . I will make you exceedingly fruitful" (Gen 17:4, 6).

This covenant with Abraham is fulfilled, of course, in the New Testament. The "nuptial union" consummated between Christ and the Church on the cross was "exceedingly fruitful" (beyond all imagining), making "the woman" at the foot of the cross the "mother of all the living." If you're familiar with my lectures and written works, you've heard me cite Archbishop Fulton Sheen explaining this great mystery as follows:

> Now we've always thought, and rightly so, of Christ the Son on the cross and the mother beneath him. But that's not the complete picture. That's not the deep understanding. Who is our Lord on the cross? He's the new Adam. Where's the new Eve? At the foot of the cross . . . . If Eve became the mother of the living in the natural order, is not this woman at the foot of the cross to become another mother? And so the bridegroom looks down at the bride. He looks at his beloved. Christ looks at his church. There is here the birth of the Church. As St. Augustine puts it, and here I am quoting him verbatim, "The heavenly bridegroom left the heavenly chambers, with the presage of the nuptials before him. He came to the marriage bed of the cross, a bed not of pleasure, but of pain, united himself with the woman, and consummated the union forever. As it were, the blood and water that came from the side of Christ was the spiritual seminal fluid." And so from these nuptials "Woman, there's your son," this is the beginning of the Church. (FS, p. 60).

And if it's fitting to conclude that Mary did not experience labor pains in giving birth to Christ in Bethlehem, she certainly experienced spiritual labor pains at the foot of the cross in giving new birth to us. It was then that Simeon's prophecy to Mary was fulfilled: "and you yourself a sword will pierce" (Lk 2:35).

So it is with all who are called to "missionary fruitfulness." Christ, in fact, warns the disciples of the suffering they will endure in precisely these terms: "When a woman is in labor, she is in anguish because her hour has arrived; but when she has given birth to a child, she no longer remembers the pain because of her joy that a child has come into the world" (Jn 16:21).

Speaking of the missionary fruitfulness of St. Paul in a pre-papal essay, Pope Benedict wrote: "The success of his mission was not the fruit of a great rhetorical art or pastoral prudence; fruitfulness was tied to his suffering, to his communion in the passion with Christ . . . . A mother cannot give life to a child without suffering. Each birth requires suffering, is suffering, and becoming a Christian is a birth . . . . We cannot give life to others without giving up our own lives" (NE I.2).

As we endure these labor pains to give life to others, let us remember, as Pope Francis reminds us here, that "no generous effort is meaningless, no painful endurance is wasted" (EG 279).

FROM *THE JOY OF THE GOSPEL*

46 "Unless . . . people find in the Church a spirituality which can offer healing and liberation, and fill them with life and peace, while at the same time summoning them to fraternal communion and missionary fruitfulness, they will end up being taken in by solutions which neither make life truly human nor give glory to God" (89).

47 We need "to give priority to actions which generate new processes in society and engage other persons and groups who can develop them to the point where they bear fruit in significant historical events. Without anxiety, but with clear convictions and tenacity" (223).

48 Trust in God's timing "enables us to work slowly but surely, without being obsessed with immediate results. It helps us patiently to endure difficult and adverse situations, or inevitable changes in our plans. It invites us to accept the tension between fullness and limitation" (223).

49 Trusting God's timing in our evangelization efforts "calls for attention to the bigger picture, openness to suitable processes and concern for the long run. The Lord himself, during his earthly life, often warned his disciples that there were things they could not yet understand and that they would have to await the Holy Spirit (see Jn 16:12–13). The parable of the weeds among the wheat (see Mt 13:24–30) graphically illustrates an important aspect of evangelization: the enemy can intrude upon the kingdom and sow harm, but ultimately he is defeated by the goodness of the wheat" (225).

50 "Often it seems that God does not exist: all around us we see persistent injustice, evil, indifference and cruelty. But it is also true that in the midst of darkness something new always springs to life and sooner or later produces fruit . . . . However dark things are, goodness always re-emerges and spreads. Each day in our world beauty is born anew, it rises transformed through the storms of history . . . . Such is the power of the resurrection, and all who evangelize are instruments of that power" (276).

51 "Because we do not always see these seeds growing, we need an interior certainty, a conviction that God is able to act in every situation, even amid apparent setbacks" (279).

52 Missionary fruitfulness "is often invisible, elusive and unquantifiable. We can know quite well that our lives will be fruitful, without claiming to know how, or where, or when. We may be sure that none of our acts of love will be lost, nor any of our acts of sincere concern for others. No single act of love for God will be lost, no generous effort is meaningless, no painful endurance is wasted" (279).

53 "Sometimes it seems that our work is fruitless, but mission is not like a business transaction or investment, or even a humanitarian activity. It is not a show where we count how many people come as a result of our publicity; it is something much deeper, which escapes all measurement. It may be that the Lord uses our sacrifices to shower blessings in another part of the world which we will never visit. The Holy Spirit works as he wills, when he wills and where he wills; we entrust ourselves without pretending to see striking results. We know only that our commitment is necessary" (279).

54 "Let us learn to rest in the tenderness of the arms of the Father amid our creative and generous commitment. Let us keep marching forward; let us give him everything, allowing him to make our efforts bear fruit in his good time" (279).

55 There is "no greater freedom than that of allowing oneself to be guided by the Holy Spirit, renouncing the attempt to plan and control everything to the last detail, and instead letting him enlighten, guide and direct us, leading us wherever he wills. The Holy Spirit knows well what is needed in every time and place. This is what it means to be mysteriously fruitful!" (280)

CHAPTER 7:

ENTERING THE REALITY OF
OTHER PEOPLE'S LIVES

In Chapter 5 we observed that a person with a missionary heart doesn't look at the world through binoculars. He or she is intimately involved in the life of others, and that means having a willingness to "bleed" with others. We musn't keep the Lord's wounds at arm's length, says Pope Francis. We must be willing to touch others' wounds—if they grant us the honor of doing so—with tenderness (see EG 270).

How can we not be reminded here of Thomas reaching out to touch Christ's wounds? In the midst of his doubt—"I will not believe unless I touch his wounds"—Thomas also manifests something of utmost importance to Christian belief: the idea, as Pope Benedict puts it, "that Jesus can now be recognized by his wounds rather than by his face." The body reveals the person. After his passion, "the signs that confirm Jesus' identity are now above all his wounds, in which he reveals to us how much he loved us." In holding this, Pope Benedict insists that

Thomas "is not mistaken" (September 27, 2006).

What is true of Christ's body is true also of his Mystical Body, the Church. Our identity is revealed by our wounds, wounds that have been touched by Christ and, because of that, now reveal the hope of glory.

A true evangelist is none other than a person whose wounds have been united with Christ's wounds, and, because of that union, the evangelist's wounds are now a channel of grace and healing for others. A true evangelist is one whose wounds have been "touched" by Christ and, because of that, he now yearns to bring that same "touch" to others. When we reach out with this kind of tenderness toward others, as Pope Francis observes, "our lives become wonderfully complicated" (EG 270).

Followers of Christ are not surprised by the "bloody mess" of human lives, their own lives first of all! That's where Christ leads us when we follow him—into the bloody mess of his Passion and death. But *always* with the hope of "passing over" into glory. Evangelists not only witness to that "pass-over," but willingly accompany others through theirs, without fear of getting splashed with blood.

FROM *THE JOY OF THE GOSPEL*

56 "To be evanglizers of souls, we need to develop a spiritual taste for being close to people's lives . . . . Jesus himself is the model of this method of evangelization . . . . If he speaks to someone, he looks into that person's eyes with deep love and concern: 'Jesus, looking upon him, loved him' (Mk 10:21). We see how accessible he is, as he draws near the blind man (see Mk 10:46–52) and eats and drinks with sinners (see Mk 2:16) without worrying about being thought a glutton and a drunkard himself (see Mt 11:19). We see his sensitivity in allowing a sinful woman to anoint his feet (see Lk 7:36–50) and in receiving Nicodemus by night (see Jn 3:1–15)" (268–69).

57 We must not keep "the Lord's wounds at arm's length . . . . Jesus wants us to touch human misery, to touch the suffering flesh of others. He hopes that we will . . . enter into the reality of other people's lives and know the power of tenderness. Whenever we do so, our lives become wonderfully complicated" (270).

58 In "our dealings with the world, we [should not appear] as an

enemy who critiques and condemns . . . . Clearly Jesus does not want us to be grandees who look down upon others, but men and women of the people. This is not an idea of the Pope, or one pastoral option among others; they are injunctions contained in the word of God which are so clear, direct and convincing that they need no interpretations which might diminish their power to challenge us. Let us live them *sine glossa*, without commentaries" (271).

CHAPTER 8:
A New Language Is Needed

We must admit that our efforts to evangelize the modern world have not been very successful (to put it mildly!). If we really want to reach the men and women of our time with the Gospel, it will demand something different than what we've seen. Not a different Gospel—for "Christ is the same yesterday, today, and forever" (Heb 13:8)—but a proclamation of Christ that is "new in ardor, methods, and expression," as St. John Paul II put it (March 9, 1983).

One of the reasons for the modern crisis in faith is the fact that the Gospel has been proclaimed "in formulas that, while true, are nevertheless at the same time outmoded," observed Pope Benedict. "They no longer speak to our living situation and are often no longer comprehensible to us." Hence, we must learn how to "translate the treasure that is perceived in [our] faith . . . into the speech and thinking of our time," he said, "so that [Christ] can become present within the horizon of the secular world's understanding. That is the great task we face" (LW, pp. 63–64).

If Christ is to become present within the secular world's understanding, that will mean walking a fine line, a place of tension, between the sacred and the secular. That will mean, in some instances, using a less "religious-sounding" language so that a broader, secular audience might be reached. As Pope Benedict put it, "one has to meet one's listeners halfway, one has to speak to them in terms of their own horizon." We do this not to "stay" there, but "to open up this horizon, to broaden it, and turn our gaze toward the ultimate" (LW, p. 179).

As Pope Francis says, "If we wish to adapt to people's language and to reach them with God's word, we need to share in their lives and pay loving attention to them" (EG 158). And this means we must stretch ourselves; we must break out of our comfort zones; we must be courageous, bold, and daring. We must strive to be all things to all men, so that some might be saved (see 1 Cor 9:22).

FROM *THE JOY OF THE GOSPEL*

59 Today's "vapid and rapid cultural changes demand that we constantly seek ways of expressing unchanging truths in a language

which brings out their abiding newness. 'The deposit of faith is one thing . . . the way it is expressed is another'" (41).

60 "There are times when the faithful, in listening to completely orthodox language, take away something alien to the authentic Gospel of Jesus Christ, because the language is alien to their own way of speaking to and understanding one another. With the holy intent of communicating the truth about God and humanity, we sometimes give them a false god or a human ideal which is not really Christian. In this way, we hold fast to a formulation while failing to convey its substance" (41).

61 The "task of evangelization operates within the limits of language and of circumstances. It constantly seeks to communicate more effectively the truth of the Gospel in a specific context . . . . A missionary heart is aware of these limits and makes itself 'weak with the weak . . . everything for everyone' (1 Cor 9:12)" (45).

62 "The Church is called to be at the service of a difficult dialogue." We need an evangelization capable of reaching "the places where new narratives and paradigms are being formed, bringing the word of Jesus to the innermost soul of our cities" (74).

63 "We should not think . . . that the Gospel message must always be

communicated by fixed formulations learned by heart or by specific words which express an absolutely invariable content. This communication takes place in so many different ways that it would be impossible to describe or catalog them all . . . . The ultimate aim should be that the Gospel, as preached in categories proper to each culture, will create a new synthesis with that particular culture" (129).

64 The language we use "must be one that people understand, lest we risk speaking to a void. Preachers often use words learned during their studies and in specialized settings which are not part of the ordinary language of their hearers. These are words that are suitable in theology or catechesis, but whose meaning is incomprehensible to the majority of Christians. The greatest risk for a preacher is that he becomes so accustomed to his own language that he thinks that everyone else naturally understands and uses it. If we wish to adapt to people's language and to reach them with God's word, we need to share in their lives and pay loving attention to them" (158).

65 "At Pentecost, the Spirit made the apostles go forth from themselves and turned them into heralds of God's wondrous deeds, capable of speaking to each person in his or her own language. The Holy Spirit also grants the courage to proclaim the newness of the Gospel with boldness in every time and place, even when it meets with opposition" (259).

CHAPTER 9:
THE WAY OF BEAUTY

As we observed in Chapter 1, eros, properly understood, is our deep, inner desire for the true, the good, and the beautiful, for what philosophers call "the transcendentals." Tragically, in the modern world, the true and the good have been relativized: "That might be true (or good) for *you,* but that's not true (or good) for *me,*" people say. And that's why appealing to the true and the good typically doesn't get us far today as evangelists.

Not so with beauty. Beauty has retained its appeal. The encounter with authentic beauty, in turn, can "wake us up" also to truth and goodness, as Pope Francis helps us understand in the selection of quotes for this chapter.

What are your favorite encounters with beauty? Where do you seek it out? What are your favorite songs or stories? What art speaks to your heart? What glories of nature awaken you? It's important that we make time to encounter beauty and to lead others to do the same.

An "essential function of genuine beauty," Pope Benedict wrote, "is that it gives man a healthy 'shock,' it draws him out of himself, wrenches him away from . . . being content with the humdrum—it even makes him suffer, piercing him like a dart, but in so doing it 'reawakens' him, opening afresh the eyes of his heart and mind, giving him wings, carrying him aloft" (November 21, 2009). In this way, says the Pontifical Council for Culture, "the marvel-arousing meeting with beauty, the 'way of beauty,' can open the pathway for the search for God . . . . It invites contemporary Augustines . . . to see through perceptible beauty to eternal beauty" (VP II.1).

"Contemporary Augustines!" These are the men and women of today who, in seeking the satisfaction and beauty they crave, have exhausted the pleasures of created things—pleasures they had idolized—and are now open to *the One* who created all such pleasures in order to lead us to his own glory and bliss. St. Augustine describes the dramatic reorientation of his yearning from created beauty to uncreated beauty in this famous passage from his *Confessions:*

> Late have I loved you, O beauty ever ancient, ever new, late have I loved you! You were within me, but I was outside, and it was there that I searched for you . . . . You called, you shouted, and you broke through my defenses. You flashed, you shone, and you dispelled my blindness. You breathed your fragrance on me; I drew in breath and now I pant

for you. I have tasted you, now I hunger and thirst for more. You
touched me, and I burned for your peace (Bk 10, Chap 26, 27.37).

Those who know something of this "divine fragrance"—this pant-
ing, hunger, and thirst for more and more of the divine sweet-
ness—cannot not invite others along this way of beauty . . . this way
that, if we stay the course, leads to Beauty incarnate: Christ himself (see
AHG, pp. 200–03).

FROM *THE JOY OF THE GOSPEL*

66 "Instead of seeming to impose new obligations, [ministers of
the new evangelization] should appear as people who wish to share
their joy, who point to a horizon of beauty, and who invite others to a
delicious banquet" (15).

67 "One of the most important things is to learn how to use
images in preaching, how to appeal to imagery . . . . An attractive
image makes the message seem familiar, close to home, practical and
related to everyday life. A successful image can make people savor the
message, awaken a desire and move the will towards the Gospel" (157).

68 "Every form of catechesis would do well to attend to the 'way of beauty.' Proclaiming Christ means showing that to believe in and to follow him is . . . something beautiful, capable of filling life with new splendor and profound joy, even in the midst of difficulties. Every expression of true beauty can thus be acknowledged as a path leading to an encounter with the Lord Jesus. This has nothing to do with . . . downplay[ing] the inseparable bond between truth, goodness and beauty as a means of touching the human heart and enabling the truth and goodness of the Risen Christ to radiate within it. If, as St. Augustine says, we love only that which is beautiful, the incarnate Son, as the revelation of infinite beauty, is supremely lovable and draws us to himself with bonds of love" (167).

69 "Each particular Church should encourage the use of the arts in evangelization, building on the treasures of the past, but also drawing upon the wide variety of contemporary expressions so as to transmit the faith in a new 'language of parables.' We must be bold enough to discover new signs and new symbols, new flesh to embody and communicate the word, and different forms of beauty which are valued in different cultural settings, including those unconventional modes of beauty which may mean little to evangelizers, yet proved particularly effective for others" (167).

70 "The best incentive for sharing the Gospel comes from contemplating it with love, lingering over its pages and reading it with the heart. If we approach it in this way, its beauty will amaze and constantly excite us. But if this is to come about, we need to recover a contemplative spirit" (264).

CHAPTER 10:

INCULTURATION

"In conformity with her constant tradition, the Church receives from the various cultures everything that is able to express better the unsearchable riches of Christ," wrote St. John Paul II (FC 10). Thus, sharing the riches of Christ with others does not mean imposing a certain cultural expression of Christianity on everyone. Tragically, evangelization has far too often been tied up with a cultural imperialism that has undervalued, devalued, or even destroyed the rich cultural inheritance of certain peoples.

"The Church is catholic," observes the *Catechism*, and this means she is "capable of integrating into her unity, while purifying them, all the authentic riches of cultures" (CCC 1202). This is what Pope Francis means by "inculturating the Gospel." It's the recognition that Christ takes nothing away from our authentic humanity. He takes nothing away from the authentic riches of a culture's language, art, music, food, customs, and the like. All that is authentically human expresses Christ and Christ expresses all that is authentically human—as does his Bride, the Church. Indeed, as Pope Francis says below, these diverse riches of cultures are the "jewels" that bedeck the Bride.

Inculturation is the recognition that Christian unity does not mean uniformity, but a "unity in distinction." And this leads, as Pope Francis tells us, to "proclaiming a synthesis" in our preaching of the Gospel: a synthesis that marries what, in our fallen humanity, often seems like unlikely spouses. In Christ, God and man, heaven and earth, spirit and matter, truth and freedom, action and contemplation, joy and suffering (and many other seemingly irreconcilable realities) are married, made "one" in a fruitful "unity in distinction."

This is the eternal plan of the Father, that *all things* would be "one" in Christ, "things in heaven and things on earth," as St. Paul tells us (see Eph 1:10). And this ultimate "oneness" ("synthesization") of everything—the consummation of all that exists in heaven and earth—is foretold and foreshadowed in our creation as male and female and the consummation of spouses in "one flesh." This is a "great mystery," says the apostle Paul, and it refers to Christ and the Church (see Eph 5:31–32).

"Where your synthesis is, there lies your heart," says Pope Francis, in a remarkable turn of phrase (EG 143). If such is the case, it's clear where the heart of the author of the letter to the Ephesians lies: in the "great mystery" that synthesizes the marriage of man and woman with the marriage of Christ and the Church. This "marriage of marriages" found in Paul's letter provides a mystical insight of unfathomable depths. As St. John Paul II declared: "Saint Paul's magnificent synthesis concerning the 'great mystery' appears as the compendium or *summa*, in some sense, *of the teaching about God and man* which was brought to fulfillment by Christ" (LF 19).

Inculturation is the introduction of everything authentically human into this "synthesis," this catholic (universal) "oneness," this mystical marriage: "Christ has made all things one in himself: heaven and earth, God and man, time and eternity, flesh and spirit, person and society. The sign of this unity and reconciliation of all things in him is peace. Christ 'is our peace' (Eph 2:14)" (EG 229).

FROM *THE JOY OF THE GOSPEL*

71 "Through inculturation, the Church 'introduces peoples, together with their cultures, into her own community,' for 'every culture offers positive values and forms which can enrich the way the

Gospel is preached, understood, and lived.' In this way, the Church takes up the values of different cultures and becomes . . . 'the bride bedecked with her jewels' (see Is 61:10)" (116).

72 In "the evangelization of new cultures, or cultures which have not received the Christian message, it is not essential to impose a specific cultural form, no matter how beautiful or ancient it may be, together with the Gospel" (117).

73 "We should not think . . . that the Gospel message must always be communicated by fixed formulations learned by heart or by specific words which express an absolutely invariable content. This communication takes place in so many different ways that it would be impossible to describe or catalog them all . . . . The ultimate aim should be that the Gospel, as preached in categories proper to each culture, will create a new synthesis with that particular culture. This is always a slow process and at times we can be overly fearful. But if we allow doubts and fears to dampen our courage, instead of being creative we will remain comfortable and make no progress whatsoever. In this case we will not take an active part in historical processes, but become mere onlookers as the Church gradually stagnates" (129).

74 "Differences between persons and communities can sometimes prove uncomfortable, but the Holy Spirit . . . can raise up diversity, plurality and multiplicity while at the same time bringing about unity. When we, for our part, aspire to diversity, we become self-enclosed, exclusive and divisive; similarly, whenever we attempt to create unity on the basis of our human calculations, we end up imposing a monolithic uniformity. This is not helpful for the Church's mission" (131).

75 "The challenge of an inculturated preaching consists in proclaiming a synthesis, not ideas or detached values. Where your synthesis is, there lies your heart. The difference between enlightening people with a synthesis and doing so with detached ideas is like the difference between boredom and heartfelt fervor. The preacher has the wonderful but difficult task of joining loving hearts, the hearts of the Lord and his people" (143).

76 "Each particular Church should encourage the use of the arts in evangelization, building on the treasures of the past but also drawing upon the wide variety of contemporary expressions so as to transmit the faith in a new 'language of parables.' We must be bold enough to discover new signs and new symbols, new flesh to embody and communicate the word, and different forms of beauty which are valued in

different cultural settings, including those unconventional modes of beauty which may mean little to the evangelizers, yet prove particularly attractive for others" (167).

77 "Christ has made all things one in himself: heaven and earth, God and man, time and eternity, flesh and spirit, person and society. The sign of this unity and reconciliation of all things in him is peace. Christ 'is our peace' (Eph 2:14)" (229).

CHAPTER 11:
SPIRIT-FILLED EVANGELIZATION

If evangelization means bringing Christ to the world, Mary was the first evangelist. How did she do it? How did she bring Christ to the world? The Holy Spirit came upon her and she conceived (see Lk 1:34–35). The Holy Spirit—the fire of God—is the very source of evangelization. Hence, the new evangelization is simply impossible, as Pope Francis tells us, "unless the fire of the Holy Spirit burns in our hearts" (EG 261).

You're probably familiar with those icons of Pentecost in which the apostles are gathered with Mary and little candle flames float above their heads symbolizing the "tongues of fire" that descended upon them. A "tongue of fire," however, is not a little candle flicker. It's more like the fiery blast of a flamethrower. This is the *fire of God* we're talking about here—something infinite, something hotter than the sun!

Let's put that in perspective. Imagine you were gathered around a campfire so hot that you had to stand about twenty feet away from it so you didn't get burned. That's a pretty big fire. Now imagine a fire so big you had to stand a hundred feet away . . . then a mile away. That's an enormous fire. Keep going ten miles . . . then a hundred miles. How big a fire are we talking about now? And that's nothing compared to the sun—a fire we have to stand ninety-three million miles away from so as not to be burnt to a crisp. And that's only a created image of the "consuming fire" that is God.

Christ came to set the world ablaze with divine fire (see Lk 12:49). And, if we are to become true evangelists, we must not fear to subject our entire being to this divine inferno. Only in this way can we share the divine life with others: we must be set ablaze by the Spirit! "As the fire transforms into itself everything it touches, so the Holy Spirit transforms into the divine life whatever is subjected to his power" (CCC 1127).

Indeed, if we are to become true evangelists, we must allow ourselves to become "wholly possessed" by the Holy Spirit (see NMI 33). Unfortunately, we hear the word "possessed" and we tend to think of something demonic. Possession by unholy spirits is, in fact, a diabolic mockery of possession by the Holy Spirit.

This is what happened to Mary when she conceived Christ: she became "wholly possessed" by the Spirit of God. She became "clothed with the sun" (Rev 12:1). This, too, is what happened to the apostles on Pentecost day. This, too, is what we must allow to happen to us. Come, Holy Spirit, come! Possess us body and soul and teach us what it means to utterly surrender to your inspiration, vibrating at your touch, set ablaze by the divine love inferno and ready to go wherever you lead us.

FROM *THE JOY OF THE GOSPEL*

78 Evangelizers must be "fearlessly open to the working of the Holy Spirit. At Pentecost, the spirit made the apostles go forth from themselves and turned them into heralds of God's wondrous deeds capable of speaking to each person in his or her own language. The Holy Spirit also grants the courage to proclaim the newness of the Gospel with boldness in every time and place, even when it meets with opposition" (259).

79 "How I long to find the right words to stir up enthusiasm for a new chapter of evangelization full of fervor, joy, generosity, courage, boundless love and attraction! Yet I realize that no words of encouragement will be enough unless the fire of the Holy Spirit burns in our hearts" (261).

80 "Spirit-filled evangelizers are evangelizers who pray and work. Mystical notions without a solid social and missionary outreach are of no help to evangelization, nor are dissertations or social or pastoral practices which lack a spirituality which can change hearts" (262).

81 "Keeping our missionary fervor alive calls for firm trust in the Holy Spirit . . . . It is true that this trust in the unseen can cause us to feel disoriented: it is like being plunged into the deep and not knowing what we will find. I myself have frequently experienced this. Yet there is no greater freedom than that of allowing oneself to be guided by the Holy Spirit, renouncing the attempt to plan and control everything to the last detail, and instead letting him enlighten, guide and direct us, leading us wherever he wills. The Holy Spirit knows well what is needed in every time and place. This is what it means to be mysteriously fruitful!" (280).

PART II:
PASTORAL PRIORITIES AND CHALLENGES

CHAPTER 12:
THE DIGNITY OF THE PERSON

The pastoral priority of the Church is to uphold the dignity of every human person in every situation. This dignity rests above all on the fact that the human person is loved eternally by God and called to everlasting communion with him (see CCC 27).

When God himself took flesh in the womb of Mary, humanity and divinity were wed in an unbreakable embrace and the dignity of man was raised to unimaginable heights. St. John Paul II wrote that the Incarnation reveals a "new anthropology"—a new understanding of what it means to be human—"which sheds light on the greatness of human nature as reflected in Christ. In him, human nature reaches its highest point of union with God." It is not possible "for human thought to conceive of a closer union with the divinity" (SP, p. 209).

Only in Christ are we able to see our own dignity and destiny: "The truth is that only in the mystery of the incarnate Word does the mystery of man take on light . . . . Christ, the final Adam by the revelation of the mystery of the Father and his love, fully reveals man to himself and makes his supreme calling clear" (GS 22). This dignity and destiny—eternal bliss with "nuptial union" with God—fills the Church with profound amazement at the human being. "In reality," wrote St. John Paul II, "the name for that deep amazement at man's worth and dignity is the Gospel, that is to say: the Good News. It is also called Christianity" (RH 10).

What a remarkable proclamation: Christianity *is* deep amazement at man's worth and dignity. "This amazement determines the Church's mission in the world" (RH 10). To be a Christian evangelist means nothing other than spreading this deep amazement at man's worth and dignity to the ends of the earth: it is to share with others the astounding truth of who they really are, why they are here, and what they are destined for.

But here we must be careful not to think of "man's dignity" abstractly. Each and every person—even those who annoy us or hurt us the most—has an infinite dignity. To make this truth the foundation for the way we act concretely toward others, toward every person we know and every person we encounter, we must "break down walls," says Pope Francis, and fill our hearts "with faces and names" (EG 274). As we do, "our lives become wonderfully complicated" (EG 270).

FROM *THE JOY OF THE GOSPEL*

82 "To believe in a Father who loves all men and women with an infinite love means realizing that 'he thereby confers upon them an infinite dignity.' To believe that the Son of God assumed our human flesh means that each human person has been taken up into the very heart of God. To believe that Jesus shed his blood for us removes any doubt about the boundless love which ennobles each human being" (178).

83 "The dignity of the human person and the common good rank higher than the comfort of those who refuse to renounce their privileges" (218).

84 "Even people who can be considered dubious on account of their errors have something to offer which must not be overlooked" (236).

85 "Every human being is the object of God's infinite tenderness, and he himself is present in their lives. Jesus offered his precious blood on the cross for that person. Appearances notwithstanding, every person is immensely holy and deserves our love. Consequently, if I can help at least one person to have a better life, that already justifies the offering of my life . . . . We achieve fulfillment when we break down walls and our heart is filled with faces and names!" (274)

CHAPTER 13:
MARRIAGE AND THE FAMILY

Our creation as male and female and the call of the two to become "one flesh" is not merely a metaphor for Christ's relationship to us. As St. John Paul II affirmed, it's the foundational way in which that eternal mystery of love becomes "visible" to us (see TOB 19:4, 95b:6). As Pope Francis observes, at "the very heart of the Gospel is life in community" (EG 177), and the fundamental human community is that of man and woman in "one flesh."

Perhaps this is why sexuality, marriage, and the family are under such violent attack today. Perhaps behind it all there is an enemy aiming all his arrows at the very foundation of human life, of the Church, and of civilization itself.

Social re-engineers do not like this fact, but when we let the data speak, it's clear: civilization rests on the family—that is, on the committed union of a man and a woman and their naturally resulting offspring. But family life of this kind is only possible to the extent that we undertake the often difficult project of *civilizing* our sexual desires, orienting them toward upholding the dignity of the human person, the truth of selfless love, and the grandeur of procreation.

When the indulgence of sexual desire becomes an end in itself, society becomes utilitarian. You are valued if you are useful. And, in this case, you are "useful" if you are sexually stimulating. If you are not, or if you get in the way of my pleasure, you will be ignored, discarded, maybe even exterminated. When pleasure is the main goal of sex, people become the means and babies become the obstacle. So we take our pleasure and we kill our offspring—and anything that gets in the way of my "right" to indulge libido (however I desire and without consequence or responsibility) is anathema.

This is not some dire prediction of an apocolyptic future. *This is the world we live in now.* Without a return to our senses, only societal chaos and collapse can result. But if a selfish "me" approach to sex spells societal breakdown, selfless sexuality (borrowing an acronym from Father Stan Fortuna) spells F.A.M.I.L.Y.—**F**orget **A**bout **M**e, **I L**ove **Y**ou.

Two thousand years ago, the first evangelization transformed civilization by showing the world an alternative to self-centered sexuality and the infanticide and cultural breakdown that inevitably results. By following Christ's example of selfless love—"Husbands, love your wives as Christ loved the Church" (Eph 5:25)—early Christians transformed the world by witnessing to the true meaning of sexuality, marriage, and family. We can *and must* do the same in the new evangelization.

FROM *THE JOY OF THE GOSPEL*

86 (Quoting St. John Paul II) "'New patterns of behavior are emerging as a result of over-exposure to the mass-media . . . . As a result, the negative aspects of the media and entertainment industries are threatening traditional values, and in particular the sacredness of marriage and the stability of the family'" (62).

87 "The family is experiencing a profound cultural crisis . . . ." The "weakening of [family] bonds is particularly serious because the family is the fundamental cell of society . . . . Marriage now tends to be viewed as a form of mere emotional satisfaction that can be constructed in any way or modified at will" (66).

88 At "the very heart of the Gospel is life in community" (177).

CHAPTER 14:
INCARNATING THE GOSPEL

By definition, "human nature" is *incarnational*. It's the marriage of body and soul, of that which is physical with that which is spiritual. We are like the angels in as much as we are spiritual and we are like the animals in as much as we are bodily and sexual. But we are *not* angels trapped in sexual bodies. We are not waiting to escape the "prison of the body," as the philosopher Plato wrongly believed (and, tragically, many Christians wrongly believe). Nor are we merely animals, as the materialists believe. Rather, we share "in both orders, being composed of body and spirit" (CCC 327).

The Christian faith hinges on this incarnate definition of human nature, for Christianity is the religion of the Incarnation: the religion that rests on the belief that God has wed himself to human nature. God is purely spiritual in his divine nature, and, as such, invisible. Yet, "in the body of Jesus 'we see our God made visible and so are caught up in love of the God we cannot see'" (CCC 477).

"The body, in fact, and only the body, is capable of making visible what is invisible: the spiritual and the divine," wrote St. John Paul II. The very purpose of the body is "to transfer into the visible reality of the world the mystery hidden from eternity in God, and thus to be a sign of it" (TOB 19:4).

Remarkable: our bodies were created by God to be a sign of his own eternal mystery of life-giving love! And this is what it means to "incarnate the Gospel." We are called to love as Jesus loves—in the flesh. As Pope Francis insists, this incarnate "principle of reality . . . is essential to evangelization" (EG 233).

One of the greatest dangers facing the Church today is the "disincarnation" of our faith. It's an attitude and approach to life that seeks to split body and soul in an attempt to "free" the soul from what many (wrongly!) consider the "unflattering" and "unholy" realities of the body and the physical world. But it's a deadly deception.

Deadly? Isn't that a bit of an exaggeration?

Well, there's a technical, theological term for the separation of body and soul. Perhaps you've heard of it—*death!* A disincarnate faith is a *dead* faith. But our faith is an incarnate, fleshy, *Gospel of life!* Christ came in the flesh that we might have life in our flesh—a flesh once bound for death, but now destined for life to the full in Christ.

"We need to bring this *Gospel of life* to the heart of every man and woman and to make it penetrate every part of society," wrote St. John

Paul II. "This involves above all proclaiming *the core* of this Gospel. It is the proclamation of a living God who is close to us [in the flesh!], who calls himself to profound communion with us [in the flesh!], and awakens in us the certain hope of eternal life [in the flesh!]. It is the affirmation of the inseparable connection between the person, his life and his bodiliness" (EV 81).

FROM *THE JOY OF THE GOSPEL*

89 Some "people want a purely spiritual Christ, without flesh and without the cross." They try to satisfy their thirst for God "with a disembodied Jesus who demands nothing of us with regard to others . . . . Genuine forms of popular religiosity are incarnate, since they are born of the incarnation of Christian faith in popular culture. For this reason, they entail a personal relationship, not with vague spiritual energies or powers, but with God, with Christ, with Mary, with the saints. These devotions are fleshy, they have a face" (88–90).

90 "To believe that the Son of God assumed our human flesh means that each human person has been taken up into the very heart of God. To

believe that Jesus shed his blood for us removes any doubt about the boundless love which ennobles each human being" (178).

91 Our "brothers and sisters are the prolongation of the incarnation for each of us." The "clearest sign for discerning spiritual growth" is the extent to which we are "going forth from ourselves toward our brothers and sisters" (179).

92 "We incarnate the duty of hearing the cry of the poor when we are deeply moved by the suffering of others" (193).

93 "Christ has made all things one in himself: heaven and earth, God and man, time and eternity, flesh and spirit, person and society. The sign of this unity and reconciliation of all things in him is peace. Christ 'is our peace.' (Eph 2:14)" (229).

94 "Realities are greater than ideas. This principle has to do with incarnation of the word and its being put into practice: 'By this you know the Spirit of God: every spirit that confesses that Jesus Christ is come in the flesh is from God' (1 Jn 4:2). The principle of reality, of a word already made flesh and constantly striving to take flesh anew, is essential to evangelization" (233).

CHAPTER 15:

THE POOR

Pope Francis wants "a Church which is poor and for the poor. They have much to teach us," he insists. In fact, if we want to become true evangelists, we "need to let ourselves be evangelized by them . . . and to embrace the mysterious wisdom which God wishes to share with us through them" (EG 198).

What is the mysterious wisdom God wishes to share with us through the poor? Among other things, the poor teach all of us our true posture before God. The desire for Infinity that haunts our humanity makes us all beggars. No creature can satisfy his own desires. No creature can provide himself with the "living water" for which he thirsts. This places us all in a posture of *radical dependence* upon the Infinite One to grant us the gift of his own Infinity.

Humble acceptance of this unmovable truth is what Scripture calls "poverty of spirit." And Christ pronounces those who embrace their utter poverty in this regard "blessed" or "beatified"—that is, overflowing with blissful happiness. Why? Because "theirs is the kingdom of heaven," theirs is the eternal wedding feast (see Mt 5:3). Acceptance of our poverty, therefore, is the prerequisite for receiving God's wealth.

As finite creatures, the only thing we have that approaches "infinity" is our poverty, our desperate *need*. Our infinite poverty, in fact, is like a reverse image of God's Infinite richness. It's the "space" in which God can place himself in our hearts, the "chalice" in which he can pour his Infinite love. This is why the Church is always feminine, she's always the Bride, and God is always the Bridegroom. It can't be the other way around. The Bridegroom is the one who *fills* and the Bride is the one who is *filled*. To be empty, needy, and open: this is just where we need to be if we want to be filled with Infinity.

Christianity is for hungry people, poor people. It has nothing to offer those who are "rich in spirit," those who are content and self-reliant. This is why Pope Francis wants "a Church which is poor and for the poor." In other words, he wants a Church that's true to herself, that's true to the human condition, and thus open to the infinite riches God wishes to lavish upon her.

FROM *THE JOY OF THE GOSPEL*

95 "We incarnate the duty of hearing the cry of the poor when we are deeply moved by the suffering of others" (193).

96 The Gospel message about the poor "is so clear and direct, so simple and eloquent, that no ecclesial interpretation has the right to relativize it. The Church's reflection on these texts ought not to obscure or weaken their force, but urge us to accept their exhortations with courage and zeal. Why complicate something so simple . . . why cloud something so clear? We should not be concerned simply about falling into doctrinal error, but about remaining faithful to this light-filled path of life and wisdom. For 'defenders of orthodoxy are sometimes accused of passivity, indulgence, or culpable complicity regarding the intolerable situations of injustice'" (194).

97 "We may not always be able to reflect adequately the beauty of the Gospel, but there is one sign which we should never lack: the options for those who are least, those whom society discards" (195).

98 "For the Church, the option for the poor is primarily a theological category rather than a cultural, sociological, political or philosophical one." This preferential option for the poor "is understood as a 'special form of primacy in the exercise of Christian charity, to which the whole tradition of the Church bears witness' . . . . This is why I want a Church which is poor and for the poor. They have much to teach us . . . . We need to let ourselves be evangelized by them . . . . We are called to find Christ . . . and to embrace the mysterious wisdom which God wishes to share with us through them" (198).

99 "No one must say that they cannot be close to the poor because their own lifestyle demands more attention to other areas. This is an excuse commonly heard in academic, business or professional, and even ecclesial circles. While it is quite true that the essential vocation and mission of the lay faithful is to strive that earthly realities and all human activity may be transformed by the Gospel, none of us can think we are exempt from concern for the poor and for social justice" (201).

100 "Any Church community, if it thinks it can comfortably go its own way without creative concern and effective cooperation in helping the poor . . . will easily drift into a spiritual worldliness camouflaged by religious practices" (207).

CHAPTER 16:
THE WAY OF LOVE

"God created man in his own image and likeness: calling him to existence through love, he called him at the same time for love . . . . Love is therefore the fundamental and innate vocation for every human being" (FC 11).

And this is why man "cannot live without love. He remains a being that is incomprehensible for himself, his life is senseless, if love is not revealed to him, if he does not encounter love, if he does not experience it and make it his own, if he does not participate intimately in it" (RH 10).

Who would argue that we yearn for love, that we are made for love? The million-dollar question is "What is love?"

The *Catechism* says that love is the "most fundamental passion." It is "aroused by the attraction of the good. Love causes a desire for the absent good and the hope of obtaining it; this movement finds completion in the pleasure and joy of the good possessed" (CCC 1765). Right there we have a summary of the entire Christian journey—from desire to destiny; from eros to "nuptial union" with the divine. Here on earth, of course, we don't yet have the fulfillment we yearn for and its absence causes us to *ache*, to *pine* for it, to *desire* it. "Wait for the Lord. Take courage. Be stouthearted and wait for the Lord" (Ps 27:14).

If we do not believe in the "way of love," however, we will not "wait for the Lord." We'll turn from him and take the fulfillment of desire into our own hands. That's called sin. In turn, we will come to view others as *means* to our own fulfillment. We will enter into relationships with one goal: the satisfaction of *our* desires. But if our love is *only* about fulfilling ourselves, then we end up not with love, but with egoism. If we are not committed to sacrificing ourselves for the other's true good, then love as a desire degenerates into love as *use*, which is not love at all (see FTH, p. 150).

We see "love as desire" and "love as sacrifice" perfectly united and perfectly fulfilled in Jesus' gift of self on the cross. "I thirst," he says (Jn 19:28). Long before we seek to quench our thirst for love in him, it is "he who first seeks us and asks us for a drink. Jesus thirsts; his asking arises from the depths of God's desire for us" (CCC 2560). And yet his desire for us is at one and the same time his desire for our good, a good for which he was ready and willing to make the ultimate sacrifice: "No one has greater love than this, that he lay down his life for his friends"

(Jn 15:13). It's in this context that he invites us to "love one another as I have loved you" (Jn 15:12).

Desire and sacrifice come together in Christ's body "given up for us." The call to love as Christ loves is inscribed by God, in fact, right in our bodies as male and female. A man's body makes no sense by itself. Nor does a woman's. Seen in light of each other, however, we discover *"the power to express love: precisely that love in which the human person becomes a gift* and—through this gift—fulfills the very meaning of his being and existence" (TOB 15:1). All authentic love flows from this starting point, from what St. John Paul II called "the spousal meaning of the body." Indeed, every way that we learn to be a "sincere gift" to others is an expression of the body's spousal meaning: the "law of love" that God inscribed in our humanity.

This is the "way" on which Christ invites us when he says, "Come follow me." As we learn to "let our masks fall and turn our hearts back to the Lord who loves us" (CCC 2711), we feel compelled to share this "way of love" with others. "If we do not feel an intense desire to share this love"—to become a selfless "gift" to others—says Pope Francis, "we need to pray insistently that he will . . . open our cold hearts and shake up our lukewarm and superficial existence" (EG 264).

FROM *THE JOY OF THE GOSPEL*

101 "Let us ask the Lord to help us understand the law of love. How good it is to have this law! How much good it does us to love one another, in spite of everything. Yes, in spite of everything! Saint Paul's exhortation is directed to each of us: 'Do not be overcome by evil, but overcome evil with good' (Rom 12:21) . . . . We all have our likes and dislikes, and perhaps at this very moment we are angry with someone. At least let us say to the Lord: 'Lord, I am angry with this person, with that person. I pray to you for him and for her.' To pray for a person with whom I am irritated is a beautiful step forward in love, and an act of evangelization. Let us do it today! Let us not allow ourselves to be robbed of the ideal of fraternal love!" (101).

102 "Evangelization aims at a process of growth which entails taking seriously each person and God's plan for his or her life . . . . It would not be right to see this call to growth exclusively or primarily in terms of doctrinal formation. It has to do with 'observing' all that the Lord has shown us as the way of responding to his love" (160-61).

103 "To believe in a Father who loves all men and women with an infinite love means realizing that 'he thereby confers upon them an infinite dignity.' To believe that the Son of God assumed our human flesh means that each human person has been taken up into the very heart of God. To believe that Jesus shed his blood for us removes any doubt about the boundless love which ennobles each human being" (178).

104 Our "brothers and sisters are the prolongation of the incarnation for each of us." The "clearest sign for discerning spiritual growth" is the extent to which we are "going forth from ourselves toward our brother and sisters" (179).

105 "The primary reason for evanglizing is the love of Jesus which we have received, the experience of salvation which urges us to ever greater love of him . . . . If we do not feel an intense desire to share this love, we need to pray insistently that he will once more touch our hearts. We need to implore his grace daily, asking him to open our cold hearts and shake up our lukewarm and superficial existence" (264).

CHAPTER 17:
THE GAZE OF LOVE

What was it about Christ that drew people to him? A magnetic personality? Charisma? Charm? Pope Francis believes "the secret lies in the way Jesus looked at people, seeing beyond their weaknesses and failings" (EG 141).

Think of the rich young man. Even in his turning away from Christ, enamored as this young man was with wordly riches, Jesus looked at him with love (see Mk 10:21). Think of the "sinful woman" who kissed and anointed Christ's feet. When this scandalized Simon the Pharisee, Jesus looked at the woman and asked Simon, "Do you see this woman?" (Lk 7:44). The point, of course, is that Simon wasn't able to see her as Jesus did. "The Lord does not see as man sees. Man sees the outward appearance, but the Lord sees the heart" (1 Sam 16:7).

The "outward appearance" of this woman revealed that she was a "sinner." That's all that Simon the Pharisee could see, convinced as he was of his own righteousness (by virtue of which he gave himself permission to stand in judgment of others). But Jesus saw something else. He saw the person—her sufferings, her misguided longings—and his heart responded with love, with mercy, with compassion.

In my experience, my difficulty seeing "sinners" simply reflects the difficulty I have as seeing myself as someone just as desperately in need of mercy as they are. We want somehow to remain above those "really bad sinners," to put a safe distance between "us" and "them." But, as Father Simon Tugwell observes, we "are no more and no less forgivable than anyone else. If we try to privelege our claim to forgiveness, it is not forgiveness we are looking for, but some other kind of recognition." We can receive genuine forgiveness, he continues, "only if we are prepared to accept the company that forgiveness places us in" (BSCT, p. 92)—that is, in the company of sinners. That means there is no distance between "us" and "them." The ground is level at the foot of the cross (see AHG, pp. 39–40).

If we are to reach people's hearts in the new evangelization, we must first pray for eyes to *see* people's hearts. And this means being trained in what Pope Francis calls the "'art of accompaniment,' which teaches us to remove our sandals before the sacred ground of the other" (EG 169). Even in those who are "dead in their sin," we encounter Christ—Christ in the tomb, as the modern mystic Caryll Houselander put it:

"Pilgrims have traveled on foot for years to kiss the Holy Sepulchre, which is empty. In sinners we can kneel at the tomb in which the dead Christ lies" (RG, pp. 170–171)—and prayerfully await, in our "accompaniment," Christ's glorious Resurrection!

We must pray earnestly for the grace to show great reverence and compassion toward *everyone.* Being human is difficult business, and behind each person's eyes is a story that, if we know its details, would break our hearts. Only as I come to see "with the eyes of Christ," says Pope Benedict, can I give to others "the look of love which they crave" (DC 18).

FROM *THE JOY OF THE GOSPEL*

106 "One cannot but admire the resources that the Lord used to dialogue with his people, to reveal his mystery to all and to attract ordinary people by his lofty teachings and demands. I believe that the secret lies in the way Jesus looked at people, seeing beyond their weaknesses and failings" (141).

107 We must "make present the fragrance of Christ's closeness and his personal gaze. The Church will have to initiate everyone—priests,

religious and laity—into this 'art of accompaniment,' which teaches us to remove our sandals before the sacred ground of the other" (169).

108 Our "closeness and our compassionate gaze . . . heals, liberates and encourages growth in the Christian life" (169).

109 "True love is always contemplative, and permits us to serve the other not out of necessity or vanity, but rather because he or she is beautiful above and beyond mere appearances: 'The love by which we find the other pleasing leads us to offer him something freely' [Thomas Aquinas]" (199).

110 Intercessory prayer is "a prayer of gratitude to God for others . . . . Far from being suspicious, negative and despairing, it is a spiritual gaze born of deep faith which acknowledges what God is doing in the lives of others" (282).

CHAPTER 18:
SELF-EXAMINATION
OF THE CHURCH

In one of the quotes selected below, Pope Francis says he prefers a Church that is "bruised and hurting" rather than a Church that is unhealthy from "clinging to its own security" (see EG 49). It would seem, in Pope Francis's mind, that a "bruised and hurting" Church is actually a *healthy* Church. How are we to understand that? We can do so only in light of St. Paul's critical lesson that "when I am weak, then I am strong" (2 Cor 12:10).

The good news of the Gospel hinges on the truth that we don't need to hide our faults, sins, and weaknesses in order to be "lovable." Tragically, most of us absorb a very different message growing up, and it creates a rather crippling perfectionism that can infect not just individual lives, but entire families and communities. In turn, this kind of perfectionism can create a milieu within the Church utterly contrary to the Gospel.

In a grand paradox, the Gospel reveals that weaknesses do not make us weak; it's *hiding* our weaknesses, refusing to bring them into the light, and "clinging to [our] own security" that makes us weak. The light is our friend. And this means that "confession" is not just one of the seven sacraments; it's a bedrock principle of the Christian life that's meant to reverse the effect of the fall in our lives.

Since the dawn of original sin, we've been hiding from God (and one another) out of fear that we're not "lovable." Faith in God's love casts our fear (see 1 Jn 4:18), enabling us to bring our "naked" humanity—with all its blemishes and ugliness—into the light, knowing we will not be chided or rejected, but embraced, forgiven, healed, and made beautiful. "I was afraid, because I was naked; so I hid myself" is transformed into "I was at peace, because I know God loves me; so I exposed myself."

For the Church to be healthy, she must first recognize that she is "bruised and hurting." She must commit herself to ongoing self-examination and purification—both corporately and in the lives of each of her individual members. And this purification means "we personally have to pass through 'fire' so as to become fully open to receiving God," says Pope Benedict. Christ's "gaze, the touch of his heart, heals us through an undeniably painful transformation 'as through fire.' But it is a blessed pain, in which the holy power of his love sears through us like a flame, enabling us to become totally ourselves and thus totally of God" (SS 46–47).

This "flame" of love is the light into which we must bring our sins, weaknesses, faults, and failings. As we learn to do so, the very things we were most afraid of seeing about ourselves become a riverbed through which the grace of salvation flows—both to us *and* to others. *This* is how evangelization takes place, by witnessing to the truth that we are loved and lovable *in our brokenness.* As Pope Francis insists, "the Church is not a tollhouse" where we have to pay for perfection to enter in. The Church, rather, is the house of our loving Father, "where there is a place for everyone, with all their problems" (EG 47).

FROM *THE JOY OF THE GOSPEL*

111 "Let us return to a memorable text [of Pope Paul VI] which continues to challenge us. 'The Church must look with penetrating eyes within herself, ponder the mystery of her own being . . . . This vivid and lively self-awareness inevitably leads to a comparison between the ideal image of the Church as Christ envisaged her and loved her as his holy and spotless bride (see Eph 5:27), and the actual image which the Church presents to the world today . . . . This is the source of the Church's heroic and impatient struggle for renewal: the struggle to correct those flaws introduced by her members which her own self-examination, mirroring her examplar, Christ, points out to her and condemns'" (26).

112 "Frequently we act as arbiters of grace rather than its facilitators. But the Church is not a tollhouse; it is the house of the Father, where there is a place for everyone, with all their problems" (47).

113 "I prefer a Church which is bruised, hurting and dirty because it has been out on the streets, rather than a Church which is unhealthy from being confined and from clinging to its own security. I do not want a Church concerned with being at the center and which then ends by being caught up in a web of obsessions and procedures. If something should rightly disturb us and trouble our consciences, it is the fact that so many of our brothers and sisters are living without the strength, light and consolation born of friendship with Jesus Christ, without a community of faith to support them, without meaning and a goal in life. More than by fear of going astray, my hope is that we will be moved by the fear of remaining shut up within structures that give us a false sense of security, within rules that make us harsh judges, within habits which make us feel safe, while at our door people are starving and Jesus does not tire of saying to us: 'Give them something to eat' (Mk 6:37)" (49).

114 "The evils of our world—and those of the Church—must not be excuses for diminishing our commitment and our fervor . . . . Our faith is challenged to discern how wine can come from water and how wheat can grow in the midst of weeds" (84).

115 "Differences between persons and communities can sometimes prove uncomfortable, but the Holy Spirit . . . can raise up diversity, plurality and multiplicity while at the same time bringing about unity. When we, for our part, aspire to diversity, we become self-enclosed, exclusive and divisive; similarly whenever we attempt to create unity on the basis of our human calculations, we end up imposing a monolithic uniformity. This is not helpful for the Church's mission" (131).

CHAPTER 19:
THE CHURCH'S MORAL TEACHING

The section of the *Catechism* that treats questions of morality has an illuminating title. It's not: "Thou Shalt Not." Rather it's: "Life in Christ." That's *life* in Christ—he came that we might have *life*, and have it in full (see Jn 10:10). Furthermore, the first line of that section of the *Catechism* is not: "Follow all these rules or you're going to hell." Rather it's: "Christian, recognize your dignity" (CCC 1691).

Life in Christ "does not imply moralism," as Pope Benedict wrote in a pre-papal essay. In fact, "reducing Christianity to morality loses sight of the essence of Christ's message: the gift of . . . communion with Jesus and thereby with God" (NE II.1). And recall from Chapter 12 that our dignity rests above all on the fact that we are all called to communion with God (see CCC 27). God wants to live with us in an eternal embrace that the saints describe as "nuptial union."

Yes, God wants to marry us, as we've been saying throughout this book, but he doesn't want a shotgun wedding! He appeals to our freedom. He invites us to respond to his infinite love with our "yes." As the *Catechism* states, "God's free initiative demands man's free response . . . . The soul only enters freely into the communion of love" (CCC 2002). The moral life, in turn, "is a response to the Lord's loving initiative" (CCC 2062). "God has loved us first . . . . The commandments then make explicit the response of love that man is called to give to his God" (CCC 2083).

Let's put it this way. If God is singing an eternal love song to us (he is, by the way—it's called the Song of Songs!), Christian morality is nothing other than learning how to dance "in step" with that song. When Pope Francis insists that "the integrity of the Gospel message must not be deformed" by proclaiming moral norms apart from the "totality of the Christian message" of God's love for us (see EG 39), he's basically saying: "Don't insist on teaching the 'dance moves' apart from the beauty of God's love song. It's the music, after all, that inspires people to want to dance in the first place."

Specific instruction in the mechanics of the dance has its place (ask any dance instructor), but it's not what we lead with as evangelists. Evangelists are those who want first to play the music for all the world to hear! Those who are seized by the beauty of the divine love song will then want to learn—of their own free will—how to dance in step with it. Becoming excellent dancers in this sense will take "much time and patience," as Pope Francis observes (see EG 171), but the infinite beauty of the music continues to inspire us to grow in grace until we become "one" with the music itself.

How rote, how bereft of color and life would a dance be that was learned only mechanically and never by "feeling" the music? That's what Christianity becomes when we reduce it to a list of rules to follow. As a result, the very invitation to life in Christ loses all "meaning, beauty, and attractiveness" (EG 34). When we preach "mere morality," we may be preaching how to "behave," but we are not preaching the Gospel, we are not inviting people to be seized by beauty; we're not inviting them to be saints. Saints are those who have been so captivated by the beauty of the Trinity's love song that they are inwardly transformed by it.

As evangelists, we have one goal: to invite the world into this love song. "Under no circumstances can this invitation be obscured!" exclaims Pope Francis (EG 39). How do we invite people in? We must commit ourselves to the dance and become "one" with the music ourselves . . . .

FROM *THE JOY OF THE GOSPEL*

116 When "certain issues which are part of the Church's moral teaching are taken out of the context which gives them their meaning . . . the message we preach then seems identified with those secondary aspects which, important as they are, do not in and of themselves convey the heart of Christ's message. We need to be realistic and not assume that our audience understands the full background to what we are saying, or is capable of relating what we say to the very heart of the Gospel which gives it meaning, beauty and attractiveness" (34).

117 "Just as the organic unity existing among the virtues means that no one of them can be excluded from the Christian ideal, so no truth may be denied. The integrity of the Gospel message must not be deformed. What is more, each truth is better understood when related to the harmonious totality of the Christian message; in this context all of the truths are important and illumine one another" (39).

118 "When preaching is faithful to the Gospel, the centrality of certain truths is evident and it becomes clear that Christian morality is not a form of stoicism, or self-denial, or merely a practical philosophy or a catalog of sins and faults. Before all else, the Gospel invites us to respond to the God of love who saves us, to see God in others and to go forth from ourselves to seek the good of others. Under no circumstance can this invitation be obscured! All of the virtues are at the service of this response of love. If this invitation does not radiate forcefully and attractively, the edifice of the Church's moral teaching risks becoming a house of cards, and this is our greatest risk. It would mean that it is not the Gospel that is being preached, but certain doctrinal or moral points based on specific ideological options. The message will run the risk of losing its freshness and will cease to have 'the fragrance of the Gospel'" (39).

119 "As the bishops of the United States of America have rightly pointed out, while the Church insists on the existence of objective moral norms which are valid for everyone, 'there are those in our culture who portray this teaching as unjust, that is, as opposed to basic human rights . . . .' We are living in an information-driven society which bombards us indiscriminately with data . . . which leads to remarkable superficiality in the area of moral discernment. In response, we need to provide an education which teaches critical thinking and encourages the development of mature moral values" (64).

120 At times "we wonder if God is demanding too much of us, asking for a decision which we are not yet prepared to make. This leads many people to stop taking pleasure in the encounter with God's word; but this would mean forgetting that no one is more patient than God our Father, that no one is more understanding and willing to wait. He always invites us to take a step forward, but does not demand a full response if we are not yet ready. He simply asks that we sincerely look at our life and present ourselves honestly before him, and that we be willing to continue to grow, asking from him what we ourselves cannot as yet achieve" (153).

121 "As for the moral component of catechesis . . . it is helpful to stress again the attractiveness and the ideal of a life of wisdom, self-fulfillment and enrichment. In the light of that positive message, our rejection of the evils which endanger that life can be better understood. Rather than experts in dire predictions, dour judges bent on rooting out every threat and deviation, we should [be] joyful messengers of challenging proposals, guardians of the goodness and beauty which shine forth in a life of fidelity to the Gospel" (168).

122 We need "'a pedagogy which will introduce people step by step to the full appropriation of the mystery.' Reaching a level of maturity where individuals can make truly free and responsible decisions calls for much time and patience . . . . The Gospel tells us to correct others and to help them to grow on the basis of a recognition of the objective evil of their actions (see Mt 18:15), but without making judgments about their responsibility and culpability (see Mt 7:1; Lk 6:37)" (171-72).

123 "Although it sounds obvious, spiritual accompaniment must lead others ever closer to God . . . . To accompany [others] would be counterproductive if it became a sort of therapy supporting their self-absorption and ceased to be a pilgrimage with Christ the Father" (170).

124 "Among the vulnerable for whom the Church wishes to care with particular love and concern are unborn children, the most defenseless and innocent among us. Nowadays efforts are made to deny them their human dignity and to do with them whatever one pleases, taking their lives and passing laws preventing anyone from standing in the way of this. Frequently, as a way of ridiculing the Church's effort to defend their lives, attempts are made to present her position as ideological, obscurantist and conservative. Yet this defense of unborn life is closely linked to the defense of each and every other human right. It involves the conviction that a human being is always sacred and invio-lable, in any situation and at every stage of development. Human beings are ends in themselves and never a means of resolving other problems. Once this conviction disappears, so do solid and lasting foundations for the defense of human rights" (213).

125 "Precisely because [Church teaching on abortion] involves the consistency of our message about the value of the human person, the Church cannot be expected to change her position on this ques-tion. I want to be completely honest in this regard. This is not some-thing subject to alleged reforms or 'modernizations.' It is not 'progres-sive' to try to resolve problems by eliminating a human life. On the other hand, it is also true that we have done little to adequately accom-pany women in very difficult situations, where abortion appears as a quick solution to their profound anguish, especially when the life developing within them is the result of rape or a situation of extreme poverty. Who can remain unmoved before such painful situations?" (214).

126 We must reject "angelic forms of purity [and] ethical systems bereft of kindness" (231).

CHAPTER 20:
TEMPTATIONS FELT BY PASTORAL WORKERS

I have been a full-time "pastoral worker" in the new evangelization since the early 1990s. More often than not, I've honestly been able to say I have the best "job" in the world: I get to invite hungry people to a banquet. Still, over the years I have encountered in myself—and in others I've worked with—every temptation about which Pope Francis warns pastoral workers. The fruit of these temptations is almost always the same: *discouragement.*

Discouragement has taken me to the verge of wanting to call it quits on more than one occasion. (Hmm, who might be the one planting seeds of discouragement in the hearts of evangelists?) I've been discouraged by the "scandal" of my own broken humanity; by the real difficulties of standing up for Christ in a hostile world; by persecutions, trials, jealousies, rivalries, slander, and betrayals; by disappointments and apostolic "failures"; by a seeming shortage of funds to carry out the work; by open dissent and rebellion among leaders in the Church; and by a host of other things. My little "escape" in those black times has been to fantasize about being a UPS driver—no cares in the world but to deliver packages, collect my paycheck, and come home to my family at the end of the day having left my work behind me. (I'm sure actual UPS drivers would tell me their job is no picnic, but I've indulged in imagining otherwise).

As Pope Francis says in one of the selected quotes from this chapter, "Keeping our missionary fervor alive calls for firm trust in the Holy Spirit, for it is he who 'helps us in our weakness' (Rom 8:26). But this generous trust has to be nourished, and we so need to invoke the Spirit constantly. He can heal whatever causes us to flag in our missionary endeavor" (EG 280). Thanks be to God!

Without fail, whenever I've invoked the Spirit in times of discouragment, I have found the strength to journey on. We shouldn't expect our trials to evaporate when we call on the Lord (that's not my experience, anyway). But with the trial, he provides a way forward so we're able to bear it. God is faithful and he will not let us be tried beyond our strength (see Cor 10:13). In fact, he empowers us with "the strength for everything" (Phil 4:13) when we trust in him.

Lord, encourage us. Revitalize us. Fill us again with your love, the love that alone compels us in the work of the new evangelization. Amen.

FROM *THE JOY OF THE GOSPEL*

127 The following list of temptations felt by pastoral workers can be found in sections 76–101 of Pope Francis's document:

- pain and shame at the sins of some members of the Church;
- inordinate concern for personal freedom and relaxation;
- heightened individualism, crisis of identity, cooling of fervor;
- inferiority complex in relation to the world leads some to hide their Christian identity;
- practical relativism: acting as if God, the poor, and the need for evangelization didn't exist;
- attachment to financial security, desire for power and human glory;
- difficulty finding trained catechists willing to persevere;
- priests who can become obsessed with protecting their free time;
- pastoral acedia (sloth);
- "tomb psychology" that turns Christians into mummies in a museum;
- a defeatism that turns us into "sourpusses";
- spiritual "desertification": like ground sterile from over-exploitation;
- "spiritual worldliness" fueled by a purely subjective faith and by self-reliance, and;
- warring among ourselves often fueled by envy and jealousy.

128 "I am aware that we need to create spaces where pastoral workers can be helped and healed, 'places where faith itself in the crucified and risen Jesus is renewed, where the most profound questions and daily concerns are shared, where deeper discernment about our experiences and life itself is undertaken in the light of the Gospel, for the purpose of directing individual and social decisions towards the good and beautiful'" (77).

129 Christ "will not deprive us of the help we need to carry out the mission which he has entrusted to us" (275).

130 "Keeping our missionary fervor alive calls for firm trust in the Holy Spirit, for it is he who 'helps us in our weakness' (Rom 8:26). But this generous trust has to be nourished, and so we need to invoke the Spirit constantly. He can heal whatever causes us to flag in our missionary endeavor" (280).

131 "It is true that this trust in the unseen [work of the Spirit] can cause us to feel disoriented: it is like being plunged into the deep and not knowing what we will find. I myself have frequently experienced this. Yet there is no greater freedom than allowing oneself to be guided by the Holy Spirit, renouncing the attempt to plan and control everything to the last detail, and instead letting him enlighten, guide and direct us, leading us wherever he wills" (280).

CHAPTER 21:
SPIRITUAL WORLDLINESS

This selection of quotes comes from what I consider the most potent section of Pope Francis's document. With the same forthrightness and "chutzpah" Christ demonstrated in confronting the pride, arrogance, and blindness of the Pharisees, Pope Francis's diagnosis unmasks and unequivocally condemns a modern "pharisaical spirit" that is rather pervasive in certain sectors of the Church today.

A "Pharisee," in this sense of the term, is one who clings rigidly to orthodox doctrine without a transformation of the heart. It's a religiosity based on "carefully cultivated appearances," and, as such, from the outside "everything appears as it should be" (EG 93). But it's a "tremendous corruption disguised as a good" (EG 97)—a worldly pride masked in "spiritual" garb. Hence, Pope Francis describes this particular sickness as "spiritual worldliness."

From a posture of religious "accomplishment" and moral "success," the spiritually worldly person permits himself to look down on every-one else's failings, while utterly unaware that his own pride and lack of charity is "infinitely more disasterous," asserts Pope Francis, than the moral failings he so readily condemns in others (see EG 93). As the parable of the tax collector and the Pharisee who "went up to the temple to pray" makes clear, things are not always as they seem in terms of who stands "justified" before God (see Lk 18:9–14). The tax collec-tors and the prostitutes enter the Kingdom ahead of the Pharisees (see Mt 21:31). Why? Because the public sinners are more readily open to God's mercy, while the self-righteous have convinced themselves they have no need of it.

More often than not, the spiritually worldly person starts with sincere motives to live a devout life and to safeguard the integrity of the Church's faith and doctrine. But, through pride, good devotion goes bad. To use Jesus' vivid description, when spiritual pride gets the best of us (and many a saint has attested that this is a very difficult sin to root out!), we become "whitewashed tombs"—nice and clean on the outside, but inside we remain full of "dead men's bones and everything unclean" (Mt 23:27).

Christ didn't come to wash our tombs on the outside. He came to raise dead men's bones to life again! But we have to be courageous enough to let Christ into the darkness of our tombs. Out of fear we cover the sin and death in our hearts with all kinds of "stones," don't we? Jesus says, "Remove the stone," and we, knowing the true state of our hearts, say, "No, Lord, there will be a stench" (see Jn 11:39). Jesus is not afraid of the stench of our hearts, the stench of our sin and shame, the stench of our pride and our death. He already sees us through the lens of what he's done for us through his own death and Resurrection. And so, when we break open our stony hearts and pour out their contents to Christ, he receives them just like he received the sinful woman's heart: like so much glorious perfume poured out upon him (see Lk 7:38, Jn 12:3). What smells like sewage to us, smells like so much "henna and nard, nard and saffron, calamus and cinnamon" (Song 4:14) to the Bridegroom. He wants—*yearns!*—for us to pour out the contents of our hearts upon him . . . so he can save us!

As we read through this chapter, we may well recognize inside ourselves the "spiritual worldliness" of which Pope Francis speaks. If so, let us allow it to be an opportunity for conversion, repentance, and growth in humility. If so, let us have the courage to come into Christ's merciful gaze.

"Before his gaze all falsehood melts away," observes Pope Benedict. "All that we build during our lives can prove to be mere straw, pure bluster, and it collapses." But here's the good news: "in the pain of this encounter, when the impurity and sickness of our lives become evident to us, there lies salvation" (SS 47).

FROM *THE JOY OF THE GOSPEL*

132 "Spiritual worldliness . . . is what the Lord reprimanded the Pharisees for . . . . It takes on many forms, depending on the kinds of persons and groups into which it seeps. Since it is based on carefully cultivated appearances, it is not always linked to outward sin; from without, everything appears as it should be. But if it were to seep into the Church, 'it would be infinitely more disastrous than any other worldliness which is simply moral'" (93).

133 We can recognize a self-absorbed promethean neopelagianism [in] those who ultimately trust only in powers and feel superior to others because they observe certain rules or remain intransigently faithful to a particular Catholic style from the past. A supposed soundness of doctrine or discipline leads instead to a narcissistic and authoritarian elitism, whereby instead of evangelizing, one analyzes and classifies others, and instead of opening the door to grace, one exhausts his or her energies in inspecting and verifying. In neither case is one really concerned about Jesus Christ or others . . . . It is impossible to think that a genuine evangelizing thrust could emerge from these adulterated forms of Christianity" (94).

134 "In some people we see an ostentatious preoccupation for the liturgy, for doctrine and for the Church's prestige, but without any concern that the Gospel have a real impact on God's faithful people and the concrete needs of the present time. In this way, the life of the Church turns into a museum piece or something which is the property of a select few . . . . The mark of Christ, incarnate, crucified and risen, is not present; closed and elite groups are formed, and no effort is made to go forth and seek out those who are distant or the immense multitudes who thirst for Christ" (95).

135 "Those who have fallen into [spiritual] worldliness look on from above and afar, they reject the prophecy of their brothers and sisters, they discredit those who raise questions, they constantly point out the mistakes of others and they are obsessed by appearances. Their hearts are open only to the limited horizon of their own immanence and interests, and as a consequence they neither learn from their sins nor are they genuinely open to forgiveness. This is a tremendous corruption disguised as a good . . . . God save us from a worldly Church with superficial spiritual and pastoral trappings!" (97).

136 "Spiritual worldliness leads some Christians to go to war with other Christians who stand in the way of their quest for power, prestige, pleasure and economic security. Some are even no longer content to live as part of the greater Church community but stoke a spirit of exclusivity, creating an 'inner circle.' Instead of belonging to the whole Church in all of its rich variety, they belong to this or that group which thinks itself different or special . . . . Beware of the temptation of jealousy! We are all in the same boat and headed to the same port! Let us ask for the grace to rejoice in the gifts of each, which belong to us all" (98–99).

137 "It always pains me greatly to discover how some Christian communities, and even consecrated persons, can tolerate different forms of enmity, division, calumny, defamation, vendetta, jealousy and the desire to impose certain ideas at all costs, even to persecutions which appear as veritable witch hunts. Whom are we going to evangelize if this is the way we act?" (100).

CHAPTER 22:
CONCERN FOR CREATION

As we discussed in Chapter 14, one of the greatest dangers facing the Church today is the "dis-incarnation" of our faith, the separation of spirit and matter. This has vast implications not only for the way we understand and approach human life, but also for the way we understand and approach the whole physical world. The Catholic-sacramental-incarnational understanding of the human being and of creation has this truth at its foundation: matter matters!

Before sin, man and woman were both "naked without shame" (see Gen 2:25). This "original acceptance of the body," wrote St. John Paul II, "was in some sense the basis of the acceptance of the whole visible world" (TOB 27:3), for man "sums up in himself the elements of the material world" (CCC 364). Since the dawn of sin, however, shame has made it very difficult for us to appreciate the goodness of the body. Rather than embracing the hard work of reclaiming that goodness, a false "spirituality" often creeps in that breeds suspicion toward the body and, in turn, toward the whole physical world. Hence, on "many occasions the Church has had to defend the goodness . . . of the physical world" (CCC 299) and call men and women to "a religious respect for the integrity of creation" (CCC 2415).

We know a disincarnate spirituality has sunk deep roots when concern for animals or for the environment comes to be labeled solely as the "unspiritual domain" of those with "less than" or even "anti" Christian sentiments. While it's true that those with otherwise anti-Christian sentiments are often concerned about the human treatment of animals and the environment, it is certainly not true that Christians should not be concerned about the same. Although we should not attribute to animals the rights and affection due only to persons, we do owe them kindness, care, and respect. In this regard, the *Catechism* reminds us of the witness of saints such as Francis of Assisi and Philip Neri (see CCC 2416).

Respect for all God's creatures flows from a proper understanding of creation and redemption. Christ came not just to "save souls" but to redeem our bodies and, through that, to restore all of creation to the purity of its origins (see CCC 2336). Working for this universal restoration—both in the "groanings" of prayer and in active responsibility for the world and its resources—is the business of every Christian: "For creation awaits with eager expectation the revelation of the children of God . . . in hope that creation itself would be set free from slavery to corruption and share in the glorious freedom of the children of God. We know that all of creation is groaning in labor pains even until now; and not only that, but we ourselves, who have the first fruits of the spirit, we also groan within ourselves as we wait for . . . the redemption of our bodies. For in this hope we were saved" (Rom 8:19–24).

In this hope—hope of the redemption of our bodies—we are reconciled not only to God, but also within ourselves as a body and soul, with one another, with the Church, and with all of creation (see CCC 1469).

FROM *THE JOY OF THE GOSPEL*

138 The "principle of universality [is] intrinsic to the Gospel, for the Father desires the salvation of every man and woman, and his saving plan consists in 'gathering up all things in Christ, things in heaven and things on earth' (Eph 1:10). Our mandate is to 'go into all the world and proclaim the good news to the whole creation' (Mk 16:15)" (181).

139 "We love this magnificent planet on which God has put us, and we love the human family which dwells here, with all its tragedies and struggles, its hopes and aspirations, its strengths and weaknesses. The earth is our common home and all of us are brothers and sisters" (183).

140 "Thanks to our bodies, God has joined us so closely to the world around us that we can feel the desertification of the soil almost as a physical ailment, and the extinction of the species as a painful disfigurement" (215).

CHAPTER 23:
MARY

It has become something of a tradition to end papal documents by turning to Mary. Hence, like his predecessors before him, Pope Francis ends *The Joy of the Gospel* with a reflection on the Mother of God.

What can we say of Mary? She is the most beautiful of all God's creatures, the sole boast of the human race. In her we see the fulfillment of rightly ordered eros, of human desire for Infinity being forever filled with the Infinite. In her, we see the embodiment of the bride, who, representing the whole human race, gave her "yes" to God's marriage proposal with such totality that she literally conceived eternal life in her womb. In Mary, we see the ecstasy to which we are all called in the eternal wedding feast. In her, we see the City of God, the gates of heaven opened, the "holy of holies," the "bridal chamber" where the marriage of heaven and earth is forever consummated!

When we understand the indispensable and unrepeatable role Mary plays in salvation history, in keeping with the Tradition of the Church, we recognize whispers of this "woman" throughout Scripture. She's foreshadowed by Eve and all the noble women of the Old Testament; she's spoken of in the law and the prophets; she's seen in the wisdom literature and in the Song of Songs; she's seen as the fulfillment of the Ark of the Covenant, the tabernacle, the tent, the temple, the house of the Lord. Thus, to "enter the courts of the Lord," is—in the deep, mystical sense of Scripture to which the Church invites us—to enter the mystery of Mary. For she is the Lord's dwelling place; she is the "City of God"; she is the embodiment of the "land" espoused by God (see Is 62:4); she is the "fertile soil" in which the Word of God takes root and produces an abundant harvest (see Ps 67:7, Mt 13:8).

When our eyes are opened to these mystical treasures, we cannot but see the mystery of Mary "everywhere" in Scripture:

> Glorious things are said of you, O City of God!
> Glorious things are said of you, dwelling place of the Most High!
> Better is one day in your courts, O Lord, than thousands elsewhere!
> I would rather rest at your gates than dwell in the tents of the wicked . . .
> One thing I ask, this alone I seek, to dwell in the house of the Lord all
>   my days,
> to gaze on the beauty of the Lord and contemplate his temple . . .
>   (see Psalms 27, 84, 87)

"Without Mary we could never truly understand the spirit of the new evangelization," says Pope Francis (EG 284). That "spirit" is none other than the Holy Spirit, the eternal, immortal seed of God that "fell like dew from heaven" upon the fertile soil of Mary's "garden" (see Lk 1:34–35, Mk 4:8). The divine wind "blows where it wills," as Jesus said (Jn 3:8), and we know that it wills to blow on Mary! The Church hears Mary's response to this mysterious wind in these famous words of the bride in Song of Songs: "Awake, O north wind, and come, O south wind! Blow upon my garden, let its fragrance be wafted abroad. Let my beloved come to his garden, and eat its choicest fruits" (Song 4:16).

St. Louis de Montfort tells us that within Mary's fertile garden there are "untold riches, beauties, rarities, and delights . . . . There are flowerbeds . . . diffusing a fragrance which delights even the angels" (TD 261). As the followers of Christ, we too are called to enter this "garden of fertile delights" and be "born again" of Mary, our spiritual mother (see Jn 3:3–13). This is how we become true apostles of the new evangelization: we must sell everything and buy the fertile field (Mary) in which the treasure of Christ is buried (see Mt 13:44). And we must dwell permanently in this "new Eden," this "paradise of delights."

"But how difficult it is for us sinners to have the freedom, the ability and the light to enter such an exalted and holy place," remarks de Montfort (TD 263). "Some," he says, "—the great majority—will stop short at the threshold and go no further. Others—not many—will take but one step into its interior. Who will take a second step? Who will take a third? Finally who will remain in it permanently" (TD 119)? "That soul will find God alone in his most glorious garden" (SM, p. 17).

Mary, star of the New Evangelization and Ravisher of Hearts, pray we have the grace to enter your most glorious garden, find God there, and share the infinite treasure we have found with the world. Amen.

FROM *THE JOY OF THE GOSPEL*

141 "With the Holy Spirit, Mary . . . made possible the missionary outburst which took place at Pentecost. She is the Mother of the Church which evangelizes and without her we could never truly understand the spirit of the new evangelization" (284).

142 "Jesus left us his mother to be our mother. Only after doing so did Jesus know that 'all was now finished' (Jn 19:28)" (285).

143 (Quoting Blessed Isaac of Stella) "'Christ dwelt for nine months in the tabernacle of Mary's womb. He dwells until the end of the ages in the tabernacle of the Church's faith'" (285).

144 "At the foot of the cross, at the supreme hour of the new creation, Christ led us to Mary . . . this icon of womanhood" (285).

145 Mary "is the friend who is ever concerned that wine not be lacking in our lives" (286).

146 Mary "is the woman whose heart was pierced by a sword and who understands all our pain" (286).

147 "Mary let herself be guided by the Holy Spirit on a journey of faith toward a destiny of service and fruitfulness . . . . Along this journey of evangelization we will have our moments of aridity, darkness, and even fatigue. Mary herself experienced these things" (287).

148 "There is a Marian 'style' to the Church's work of evangelization. Whenever we look to Mary, we come to believe once again in the revolutionary nature of love and tenderness" (288).

149 "Mary is able to recognize the traces of God's Spirit in events great and small. She constantly contemplates the mystery of God in our world, in human history, and in our daily lives" (288).

150 "Mary . . . you gave yourself completely to the Eternal One . . . Mother of love, Bride of the eternal wedding feast, pray for the Church, whose pure icon you are, that she may never . . . lose her passion . . ." (288).

Thank you for spending time with

"POPE FRANCIS TO GO: BITE-SIZED MORSELS FROM THE JOY OF THE GOSPEL"

If you enjoyed and were inspired by this book, encourage others to read it by leaving a review at whatever site you purchased it (if the site doesn't have a review section, go to the Amazon page for this book).

Please check out the many other offerings by Christopher West and The Cor Project on the following pages!

THE ❤ COR PROJECT

MEMBERSHIP

oin The Cor Project and receive daily
rmation from Christopher West in the
heology of the Body.

or a full list of benefits, visit corproject.com
nd click "Cor Membership."

ORPROJECT.COM

THE COR PROJECT

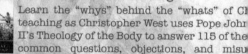

Check out these popular titles by **CHRISTOPHER WEST**

BOOKS

Fill These Hearts: God, Sex, and Universal Longing

This is a book about desire. Not just t wants or superficial cravings, but the mos powers of sexuality and spirituality that us and compel us on our search for some Along the way, *Fill These Hearts* blows t off the idea of Christianity as a repre antisex religion and unveils the hidden tr life—that the restless yearnings we feel in both our bodie our spirits are the very cry of our hearts for God.

Good News About Sex and Marri Answers to Your Honest Quest About Catholic Teaching

Learn the "whys" behind the "whats" of Cl teaching as Christopher West uses Pope John II's Theology of the Body to answer 115 of the common questions, objections, and misu standings. Chapters on divorce and annulments, prem sex, marital sex, contraception, infertility and reprodu technologies, homosexuality, and Christian celibacy Christopher to address virtually every conceivable top your education in sexual morality amounted to "Thou not," you will be blown away by the beauty and splendor "good news" that West unfolds in this book!

Theology of the Body Explained Commentary on John Paul II's *Man Woman He Created Them*

If you want to "go the distance" in understa Pope John Paul II's Theology of the Body, th the book for you. A guided tour of the late p teaching from start to finish, West's 650 "magnum opus" leaves no stone unturned. First publish 2003, it has served as a standard reference text in univers seminaries, and private study ever since. There has never a more thorough guide to the Theology of the Body.

Theology of the Body for Beginners Basic Introduction to Pope Paul Sexual Revolution

This short summary of West's 650-page comr tary is an excellent entry point into this life-ch ing vision of what makes us human. If you are to the ideas of the Theology of the Body or wa share this teaching with others who have never heard before, this is the book you're looking for.

THE COR PROJECT

CORPROJECT.COM

Invite Christopher West to speak in your area and be prepared for a life-changing experience. Here's what people are saying:

"Outstanding!"

"Riveting!"

"This is the truth that all people long to hear."

"Blown away!"

"Life-changing!"

"...speaks to the heart."

EVENT BOOKING

THE COR PROJECT

follow
CHRISTOPHER WEST

f cwestofficial

🐦 @CWestTOB

read Christopher's blog at
CORPROJECT.COM/BLO

THEOLOGY OF THE BODY

OF THE BODY

INSTITUTE

cating minds • transforming hearts • changing lives

Theology of the Body I: Head and Heart Immersion

This course examines the main themes of the 129 Wednesday audience addresses that comprise Pope John Paul II's Theology of the Body.

Theology of the Body II: Into the Deep

This course builds upon and advances the material presented in Theology of the Body I, revisiting the Wednesday audience addresses for more in-depth study. Particular focus is given to Pope John Paul II's "lost audiences" on the Song of Songs. (Requires completion of TOB I)

Theology of the Body III: The New Evangelization

This course examines the implications of Pope John Paul II's Theology of the Body for the "new evangelization." It demonstrates that the Theology of the Body is not only a teaching on sexual love, but has implications for all of theology, and provides a compelling way to present the Gospel message to the modern world. (Requires completion of TOB I and II)

Learn more and register for these courses at tobinstitute.org.